John Tufts

Pilgrim songs for the Sunday school

John Tufts

Pilgrim songs for the Sunday school

ISBN/EAN: 9783337265182

Printed in Europe, USA, Canada, Australia, Japan

Cover: Foto ©Thomas Meinert / pixelio.de

More available books at **www.hansebooks.com**

PILGRIM SONGS

FOR THE

SUNDAY SCHOOL

EDITED BY JOHN W. TUFTS

CONGREGATIONAL SUNDAY SCHOOL
AND
PUBLISHING SOCIETY

BOSTON • CHICAGO

The Congregational Sunday-School and Publishing Society takes special pleasure in presenting the "Pilgrim Songs" to the Sunday-schools of its constituency, trusting that they will find in both the hymns and tunes, and especially in their combination, a devout and helpful vehicle of praise. They are sure that the musical editing has been done with ability and conscientiousness. The selection of hymns and the preparation of the book in general has been under the supervision of the Committee on Sunday-school Publications.

S. B. CAPEN, President.

GEO. M. BOYNTON, Chairman of Committee.

PRESS OF STANLEY & USHER,
171 DEVONSHIRE STREET, BOSTON, MASS.

PREFACE.

In Sunday-schools rote singing is to a large extent unavoidable, and the melodies must be learned by imitation. To do this, let all for awhile sing the tune until it can be given with accuracy in time and freedom in movement. Let everything be sung in a spirited and elastic manner, even the so-called Chorales.

To induce a brighter and swinging motion, quarter-notes are used in preference to the usual half-notes, so that a slow and dragging style may be avoided. Few marks of expression are used, but special care has been given in the adaptation of words to the music, so that positive sympathy may be established between them.

Good music frequently needs repetition to be fully enjoyed, and this repetition may generally be taken as a test of its character. We never tire of the best melodies, and singers should not judge hastily of the excellence of any composition, for if really good it will not fail to become fixed in the memory.

Melodies from the "Great Masters" are generally fragments, made up to fit the usual forms of metre found in tune books, and thus prepared they would hardly be recognized by the original composers. In this book only those are introduced that are unmistakably in the original form, and those have been rejected that in the original form were associated with words or surroundings that would be an offence to religious feeling and good taste. The addition of sacred words does not change the real character of a melody written for other uses, and every thoughtful person will reject such "adaptations" as are too often found in books designed for use in the Church or Sunday-school. The time has certainly come when everything inappropriate, trivial, or secular, should be banished from our church music.

Good music is earnest and true, but it is by no means dull or lifeless. The heaviness too often experienced is not in the matter but in the manner, and the result of an indifferent manner is to make this part of the service distasteful.

The melodies here found are invariably simple and tuneful, such as can be easily learned by the youngest children. The varied harmonies are carefully written and adapted to the voices.

3

Children must be allowed more freedom of movement than adults. Let them sing in a bright and cheerful way, and do not let them grow weary with long and doleful sounds. The boundary of good taste need not be passed to accomplish a good result if reasonable care is exercised. It is intended that a large number shall sing the melody, especially at the outset. When the tune is thoroughly learned, the other parts may be added by those who can sing them exactly as written.

One matter is seriously urged upon the teachers. Never leave a song until every difficulty has been overcome. As the melodic character of each song has been the most important reason for its introduction, it is believed that all will readily understand and enjoy the practice. Let the music be repeated until it becomes the ready vehicle for the expression of the sentiment of the words. In this way, and in this way only, can the right feeling be made manifest.

In the Chorales the melody should be sung by all: especially is this necessary with the older ones and those of German origin. It is considered that these should be learned and known by all young singers, as they are hallowed by religious associations, and are inseparable from the Church's history since Luther's time. A few of these great melodies have been retained, especially those having a clear and decided movement, and that are in agreement with our best church music.

Appropriate selections have been made for the different parts of the school sessions and for the seasons and festivals of the year, and they are so arranged that they can be easily found as they may be required.

A short and simple service, with chanted musical responses, has been prepared for those who desire a regular form.

The musical selections have been gathered from the best sources, to which has been added much new and original matter.

Especial attention is called to the words, as these have been chosen with great care and with particular reference to their use by the younger members of the Sunday-schools.

BOSTON, November 1, 1886.   JOHN W. TUFTS.

NOTE. — *Many old and familiar hymns have received in this work new musical settings. This has been done to gain freshness and variety of music for use in the Sunday-school, as well as to bring both words and music into agreement and sympathy, this being the aim of the editor throughout the book. If the more familiar melodies are desired, they can be found in the various church collections. The school will readily sing them without the aid of notes.*

4

An Order of Exercises for Sunday-Schools.

✠ I.—WORSHIP. ✠
(All stand.)

Superintendent. — O come, let us sing unto the Lord: let us make a joyful noise to the rock of our salvation.

School. — Let us come before his presence with thanksgiving, and make a joyful noise unto him with psalms.

OPENING HYMN OF PRAISE.

(School seated.)

Superintendent. — O come, let us worship and bow down: let us kneel before the Lord our Maker.

School. — God is a Spirit: and they that worship him must worship him in spirit and in truth.

PRAYER.

SONG SERVICE.

One or more hymns may be sung.

✠ II.—INSTRUCTION. ✠
RECITATION.

The Twenty-third Psalm or the Creed repeated in unison: or the Commandments repeated, with chanted response to each, from organ and choir (or the Commandments may be repeated by the superintendent, with responses sung by the school): or the Beatitudes, the superintendent reading the blessings and the school the rewards.

LESSON READ.

Responsively, and from Bibles as far as possible.

LESSON STUDIED.

Thirty-five to forty-five minutes, with warning-bell five minutes before close.

REVIEW.

By pastor or superintendent.

LESSON HYMN.

✠ III.—BUSINESS. ✠
MISSIONARY OFFERING.

REPORT OF SECRETARY AND TREASURER.

NOTICES.

DISTRIBUTION OF LIBRARY BOOKS.

✹ IV.—CLOSING SERVICE. ✹

CLOSING HYMN.

PRAYER.

Closing with The Lord's Prayer, repeated in unison or chanted.

SUPERINTENDENT'S BLESSING.—And the very God of peace sanctify you wholly; and I pray God your whole spirit, and soul, and body, be preserved blameless unto the coming of our Lord Jesus Christ.

GLORIA PATRI.

Glory be to the *Father*;and to the	Son	*and*............	to	the	Ho - ly	Ghost;
As it was in the begin-						
ning, is *now* and.....	ev - er	shall be	*world*........	with -out	end. A -	men.

No. 1.

No. 2.

DISMISSION.

The Beatitudes.

Blessed are the poor in spirit : for theirs is the kingdom of heaven.
Blessed are they that mourn : for they shall be comforted.
Blessed are the meek : for they shall inherit the earth.
Blessed are they which do hunger and thirst after righteousness : for they shall be filled.
Blessed are the merciful : for they shall obtain mercy.
Blessed are the pure in heart : for they shall see God.
Blessed are the peacemakers : for they shall be called the children of God.
Blessed are they which are persecuted for righteousness' sake : for theirs is the kingdom of heaven.
Blessed are ye, when men shall revile you, and persecute you, and shall say all manner of evil against you falsely, for my sake.
Rejoice, and be exceeding glad : for great is your reward in heaven : for so persecuted they the prophets which were before you

6

1. Our *Father* who..... art in heaven, *hal* - - low - ed be Thy name:
2. Thy kingdom *come* Thy will be done *on*............ earth – as it is in heaven.
3. Give us this *day* our.. dai - ly bread; and forgive us our trespasses, as we forgive *those* that..... trespass a - gainst — us.

4. And lead us *not* into temp - - ta - - tion, *but* de - - liv - er us from evil;

5. For Thine is the king - dom and the power, ...

... and the glo - ry for - ev - er. A - - men.

Creed.

I believe in God the Father Almighty, Maker of heaven and earth ; and in Jesus Christ his only Son our Lord ; who was conceived by the Holy Ghost, born of the Virgin Mary, suffered under Pontius Pilate ; was crucified, dead, and buried ; the third day he rose from the dead ; he ascended into heaven, and sitteth on the right hand of God the Father Almighty ; from thence he shall come to judge the quick and the dead.

I believe in the Holy Ghost ; the Holy Catholic Church,* the communion of saints ; the forgiveness of sins ; the resurrection of the body, and the life everlasting. AMEN.

* By the Holy Catholic Church is meant the Church of God in general.

7

The Ten Commandments.

And God spake all these words, saying,

I. Thou shalt have no other gods before me.

II. Thou shalt not make unto thee any graven image, or any likeness of any thing that is in heaven above, or that is in the earth beneath, or that is in the water under the earth: thou shalt not bow down thyself to them, nor serve them: for I the Lord thy God am a jealous God, visiting the iniquity of the fathers upon the children unto the third and fourth generation of them that hate me; and shewing mercy unto thousands of them that love me, and keep my commandments.

III. Thou shalt not take the name of the Lord thy God in vain; for the Lord will not hold him guiltless that taketh his name in vain.

IV. Remember the sabbath day, to keep it holy. Six days shalt thou labour, and do all thy work: but the seventh day is the sabbath of the Lord thy God: in it thou shalt not do any work, thou, nor thy son, nor thy daughter, thy manservant, nor thy maidservant, nor thy cattle, nor thy stranger that is within thy gates: for in six days the Lord made heaven and earth, the sea, and all that in them is, and rested the seventh day: wherefore the Lord blessed the sabbath day, and hallowed it.

V. Honour thy father and thy mother: that thy days may be long upon the land which the Lord thy God giveth thee.

VI. Thou shalt not kill.

VII. Thou shalt not commit adultery.

VIII. Thou shalt not steal.

IX. Thou shalt not bear false witness against thy neighbour.

X. Thou shalt not covet thy neighbour's house, thou shalt not covet thy neighbour's wife, nor his manservant, nor his maidservant, nor his ox, nor his ass, nor any thing that is thy neighbour's.

RESPONSES TO THE COMMANDMENTS.

1 — 9. Lord have mercy upon us, and incline our hearts to | keep this | law.

AFTER THE TENTH.

Lord have mercy upon us, and write all these Thy .... laws in our hearts, we be-seech Thee.

8

PILGRIM SONGS.

1   O happy Band of Pilgrims.

1 . O hap - py band of pil-grims, If on - ward ye will tread,

With Je - sus as your Fel - low, To Je - sus as your Head.

2 O happy, if ye labor
   As Jesus did for men :
 O happy, if ye hunger
   As Jesus hungered then!

3 The trials that beset you,
   The sorrows ye endure,
   The manifold temptations
   That death alone can cure,—

4 What are they, but His jewels
   Of right celestial worth?
 What are they, but the ladder
   Set up to Heaven on earth?

5 O happy band of pilgrims,
   Look upward to the skies,
 Where such a light affliction
   Shall win you such a prize.

9

Hark! hark, my Soul.

1. Hark! hark my soul! an - gel - ic songs are swell - ing O'er earth's green
2. On - ward we go. for still we hear them sing - ing. "Come, wea - ry

fields. and o - cean's wave-beat shore: How sweet the truth those
souls. for Je - sus bids you come; And. thro' the dark its

bless-ed strains are tell - ing Of that new life when sin shall be no more.
ech - oes sweet-ly ring - ing. The mu - sic of the Gos-pel leads us home.

p CHORUS.　　　cres.

An - gels of Je - sus. an - gels of light.

Hark! hark, my Soul.—Concluded.

Sing - ing to wel-come the pil-grims of the night. Sing - ing to

wel-come the pil-grims, the pilgrims of the night. A - men. A - men.

3 Far. far away, like bells at evening pealing,
   The voice of Jesus sounds o'er land and sea.
And laden souls by thousands meekly stealing.
   Kind Shepherd. turn their weary steps to Thee.

   Angels of Jesus. &c.

4 Rest comes at length, though life be long and dreary,
   The day must dawn, and darksome night be past:
Faith's journey ends in welcome to the weary.
   And heaven, the heart's true home, will come at last.

   Angels of Jesus. &c.

5 Angels, sing on! your faithful watches keeping:
   Sing us sweet fragments of the songs above:
Till morning's joy shall end the night of weeping.
   And life's long shadows break in cloudless love.

   Angels of Jesus, &c.

3 Again the Morn of Gladness.

1. A-gain the morn of glad-ness, The morn of light is here;

And earth it-self looks fair - er, And heav'n it-self more near;

The bells, like an - gel-voi - ces, Speak peace to ev - 'ry breast;

And all the land lies qui - et, To keep the day of rest.

Again the Morn of Gladness.—Concluded.

"Glo-ry be to Je-sus!" Let all His chil-dren say:

"He rose a-gain, He rose a-gain On this glad day."

2 Again, O loving Saviour.
   The children of Thy grace.
   Prepare themselves to seek Thee
   Within Thy chosen place.
   Our songs shall rise to greet Thee,
   If Thou our hearts wilt raise :
   If Thou our lips wilt open.
   Our mouths shall show Thy praise.

   "Glory be to Jesus !" &c.

3 The shining choir of angels
   That rest not day or night.
   The crowned and palm-decked martyrs,
   The saints arrayed in white,
   The happy lambs of Jesus
   In pastures fair above,—
   There all adore and praise Him
   Whom we too praise and love.

   " Glory be to Jesus !" &c.

4 The church on earth rejoices
   To join with these to-day :
   In every tongue and nation
   She calls her sons to pray ;
   Across the northern snow-fields,
   Beneath the Indian palms.
   She makes the same pure offering.
   And sings the same sweet psalms.

   " Glory be to Jesus !"

5 Tell out, sweet bells, His praises !
   Sing, children, sing His name !
   Still louder and still farther
   His mighty deeds proclaim.
   Till all whom He redeemèd
   Shall own Him Lord and King ;
   Till every knee shall worship.
   And every tongue shall sing.

   " Glory be to Jesus !"

4 Now that the Daylight fills the Sky.

1. Now that the daylight fills the sky, We lift our hearts to God on high,
2. May He re-strain our tongues from strife, And shield from an-ger's din our life,

That He in all we do or say, Would keep us free from harm to-day.
And guard with watch-ful care our eyes From earth's ab-sorb-ing van-i-ties.

3 Oh may our inmost hearts be pure,
 From thoughts of folly kept secure;
 And pride of sinful flesh subdued,
 Through sparing use of daily food.

4 So we, when this day's work is o'er,
 And shades of night return once more,
 Our path of trial safely trod,
 Shall give the glory to our God.

5 Through the silent Hours of Night.

1. Thro' the si-lent hours of night, Safe un-til the morn-ing light,
2. Now as dawns an-oth-er day, Fa-ther, guide us on our way!

14

Through the silent Hours of Night.—Concluded.

God has kept us safe from harm, Shel-tered by His lov-ing arm.
With its gifts Thy bless-ing send, May Thy grace our steps at - tend.

3 All who love us, parents dear,
Friends whose smiles our pathway cheer,
We, this day, to Thee commend,
Bless and keep them to its end.

4 Make us loving, kind and true,
Willing each day's work to do;
Earnest to show forth Thy praise,
Through this life's remaining days.

6   Awake, my Soul, and with the Sun.

1. A-wake, my soul, and with the sun Thy dai - ly stage of du - ty run;

Shake off dull sloth, and joy - ful rise To pay thy morn-ing sac - ri - fice.

2 Wake, and lift up thyself, my heart,
And with the angels bear thy part,
Who all night long unwearied sing
High praise to the Eternal King.

3 All praise to Thee, who safe hast kept,
And hast refreshed me while I slept:
Grant, Lord, when I from death shall wake
I may of endless light partake.

4 Lord, I my vows to Thee renew;
Disperse my sins as morning dew;
Guard my first springs of thought and will,
And with Thyself my spirit fill.

5 Direct, control, suggest, this day,
All I design, or do, or say,
That all my powers, with all their might,
In Thy sole glory may unite.

15

When Morning gilds the Skies.

1. When morn-ing gilds the skies, My heart a-wak-ing cries
2. When-e'er the sweet church-bell Peals o-ver hill and dell,

May Je-sus Christ be praised: A-like at work and prayer,
May Je-sus Christ be praised: Oh hark to what it sings.

To Je-sus I re-pair: May Je-sus Christ be praised.
As joy-ous-ly it rings, May Je-sus Christ be praised.

3 Does sadness fill my mind?
　A solace here I find,
　　May Jesus Christ be praised:
　Or fades my earthly bliss?
　My comfort still is this,
　　May Jesus Christ be praised.

4 In heaven's eternal bliss
　The loveliest strain is this,
　　Let Jesus Christ be praised:
　Let earth and sea and sky
　From depth to height reply,
　　May Jesus Christ be praised.

Upraised from Sleep, to Thee we kneel.

1. Up - raised from sleep, to Thee we kneel, As day doth break; To Thee, O Lord, a - loud we sing, To Thee the song of an - gels bring; For mer - cy's sake, Oh, pi - ty take, O Ho - ly, Ho - ly, Ho - ly.

2 Thou, Lord, hast from my couch of rest
Uplifted me;
Oh, light my mind; Oh, light my heart,
And ope my lips to take their part
In praising Thee,
Blest Trin y,
O Holy, Holy Ioly.

7

Every Morning Mercies new.

1. Ev-'ry morn-ing mer-cies new Fall as fresh as ear-ly dew;

Ev-'ry morn-ing let us pay Tri-bute with the ear-ly day;

For Thy mer-cies, Lord, are sure: Thy com-pas-sion doth en-dure.

2 Still the greatness of Thy love
Daily doth our sins remove;
Daily, far as east to west
Lifts the burden from the breast;
Gives unbought to those who pray
Strength to stand in evil day.

3 Let our prayers each morn prevail,
That these gifts may never fail;
And, as we confess the sin
And the tempter's power within,
Feed us with the Bread of Life;
Fit us for our daily strife.

10   Come, my Soul, thou must be waking.

1. Come, my soul, thou must be wak-ing, Now is break-ing O'er the
2. Pray that He may pros-per ev-er Each en-deav-or, When thine

earth an-oth-er day: Come to Him who made this
aim is good and true; But that He may ev-er

splen-dor; See thou, ren-der All thy fee-ble strength can pay.
thwart thee, And con-vert thee, When thou e-vil wouldst pur-sue.

3 Think that He thy ways beholdeth,
    He unfoldeth
Every fault that lurks within;
He, the hidden shame glossed over,
    Can discover,
And discern each deed of sin.

4 Mayest thou on life's last morrow,
    Free from sorrow,
Pass away in slumber sweet;
And, released from death's dark sadness,
    Rise in gladness,
That far brighter Sun to greet.

11   Thine earthly Sabbaths, Lord, we love.

1. Thine earth - ly Sabbaths, Lord, we love; But there's a no - bler rest a-bove,
2. No more fa - tigue, no more dis-tress, Nor sin, nor death shall reach the place;

To that our long-ing souls as - pire, With cheer-ful hope and strong de-sire.
No groans shall min - gle with the songs Which war -ble from im-mor-tal tongues!

3 No rude alarms of raging foes,
No cares to break the long repose,
No midnight shade. no clouded sun,
But sacred, high, eternal noon.

4 O long expected day begin!
Dawn on these realms of woe and sin,
Thine earthly Sabbaths. Lord, we love;
But wait the nobler rest above.

12   Blest Day of God! most calm, most bright.

1. Blest day of God! most calm, most bright, The first, and best of days;
2. My Saviour's face made thee to shine; His ris - ing thee did raise,

Blest Day of God!—Concluded.

The laborer's rest, the saints de-light, The day of prayer and praise.
And made thee heavenly and di - vine Be-yond all oth - er days.

3 The first-fruits oft a blessing prove
To all the sheaves behind;
And they the day of Christ who love,
A happy week shall find.

4 This day I must with God appear;
For Lord, the day is Thine;
Help me to spend it in Thy fear,
And thus to make it mine.

13   Another six Days' Work is done.

1. An - oth - er six days' work is done; An - oth - er Sab-bath is be - gun;
2. Oh that our tho'ts and thanks may rise, As grate-ful in - cense to the skies;

Re-turn, my soul, en - joy the rest; Im-prove the day thy God hath blessed.
And draw from heaven that sweet re-pose, Which none but he that feels it knows.

3 This heavenly calm within the breast
Is the dear pledge of glorious rest,
Which for the church of God remains;
The end of cares, the end of pains.

4 In holy duties let the day,
In holy pleasures pass away;
How sweet a Sabbath thus to spend,
In hope of one that ne'er shall end.

Again returns the Day of holy Rest.

1. A - gain re - turns the day of ho - ly rest, Which, when He
made the world, Je - ho - vah blest; When, like His own, He
bade our la-bors cease. And all be pi - e - ty, and all be peace.

2 Let us devote this consecrated day
   To learn His will, and all we learn, obey,
   In pure religion's hallowed duties share,
   And join in penitence, and join in prayer.

3 Father of heaven, in whom our hopes confide,
   Whose power defends us, and whose precepts guide;
   In life our Guardian, and in death our Friend,
   Glory supreme be Thine, till time shall end.

15   O Day of Rest and Gladness.

1. O day of rest and glad - ness, O day of joy and light,
2. Thou art a cool - ing foun - tain In life's dark drear - y sand;
3. New gra - ces e - ver gain - ing From this our day of rest,

O balm of care and sad - ness, Most beau - ti - ful, most bright!
From thee, like Pis - gah's moun - tain, We view our prom - ised land;
We reach the rest re - main - ing To spir - its of the blest;

On thee the high and low - ly, Be - fore the e - ter - nal throne,
A day of sweet re - fec - tion, A day thou art of love,
And there our voice up - rais - ing To Fa - ther and to Son,

Sing Ho - ly, Ho - ly, Ho - ly, To the great Three in One.
A day of re - sur - rec - tion From earth to things a - bove.
And Ho - ly Ghost, be prais - ing Ev - er the Three in one.

23

1. Hark! hark! the or-gan
2. Hark! hark! the or-gan

loud - ly peals, Our thank-ful hearts in - vit - ing To sing our great Cre -
loud - ly peals, Our thank-ful hearts in - vit - ing To sing the praise of

Hark! hark! the Organ loudly peals.—Concluded.

- a-tor's praise, Both rich and poor u - nit - ing! Ye heav'ns and earth rejoice! And
Christ our King, Both rich and poor u - nit - ing! Who left His throne on high, And

ev - 'ry heart and voice   Your joy - ous strains upraise,   In notes of   endless
low - ly came to   die,   That we from earth might rise,   To realms beyond the

praise,   Be - fore His throne for - ev - er and for - ev - er.
skies,   And live with Him for - ev - er and for - ev - er.

17 Safely through another Week.

1. Safe - ly through an - oth - er week, God has brought us on our way;

Let us now a bless - ing seek, Wait - ing in His courts to - day;

Day of all the week the best, Em - blem of e - ter - nal rest.

2 Here we come Thy name to praise :
  Let us feel Thy presence near:
May Thy glory meet our eyes,
  While we in Thy house appear :
Here afford us. Lord, a taste
Of our everlasting feast.

3 May the gospel's joyful sound
  Conquer sinners. comfort saints.
Make the fruits of grace abound,
  Bring relief from all complaints;
Thus let all our Sabbaths prove
Till we join the church above.

18   Peace be to this Habitation.

1. { Peace be to this hab - i - ta - tion, Peace to all that dwell there-in; }
{ Peace, the earn - est of sal - va - tion, Peace, the fruit of pardoned sin; }

Peace that speaks the heav -'nly Giv - er; Peace, to world - ly minds un-known;

Peace di - vine, that lasts for - ev - er, Peace that comes from God a - lone.

2 Prince of Peace, be ever near us ;
  Fix in all our hearts Thy home:
  With Thy gracious presence cheer us ;
  Let Thy sacred kingdom come.
  Raise to heaven our expectation ;
  Give our favored souls to prove
  Glorious and complete salvation
  In the realms of bliss above.

27

19   We bring no glittering Treasures.

1. We bring no glitt'ring treasures, No gems from earth's deep mine, We come with simple measures, To chant Thy love di-vine. Children, Thy fa-vors shar-ing, Their voice of thanks would raise; Father ac-cept our off-'ring. Our song of grate-ful praise.

2 The dearest gift of heaven.
   Love's written word of truth.
To us is early given
   To guide our steps in youth ;
We hear the wondrous story,
   The tale of Calvary:
We read of homes in glory.
   From sin and sorrow free.

3 Redeemer. grant Thy blessing !
   Oh. teach us how to pray.
That each. Thy fear possessing,
   May tread life's onward way !
Then. where the pure are dwelling,
   We hope to meet again.
And. sweeter numbers swelling,
   Forever praise Thy name.

1. Lord of the worlds a - bove, How pleas - ant and how fair
2. O hap - py souls, that pray Where God ap - points to hear!

The dwell - ings of Thy love, Thine earth - ly tem - ples are!
O hap - py men, that pay Their con - stant ser - vice there!

To Thine a - bode My heart as-pires With warm desires To see my God.
They praise Thee still: And hap-py they That love the way To Zi - on's hill.

3 They go from strength to strength
   Through this dark vale of tears,
Till each arrives at length,
   Till each in heaven appears :
     O glorious seat;
     When God our King
     Shall thither bring
     Our willing feet.

4 God is our Sun and Shield,
   Our Light and our Defence;
With gifts His hands are filled,
   We draw our blessings thence;
     Thrice happy he,
     O God of Hosts,
     Whose spirit trusts
     Alone in Thee.

Lord, we come before Thee now.

1. Lord, we come be - fore Thee now; At Thy feet we hum - bly bow:
2. In Thine own ap - point - ed way, Now we seek Thee; here we stay;
3. Com - fort those who weep and mourn; Let the time of joy re - turn;

Oh, do not our suit dis - dain: Shall we seek Thee, Lord, in vain?
Lord, from hence we would not go, Till a bless - ing Thou be - stow.
Those that are cast down lift up; Make them strong in faith and hope.

Lord on Thee our souls de - pend; In com - pas - sion, now de - scend;
Send some mes - sage from Thy word, That may joy and peace af - ford;
Grant that all may seek and find Thee, a God su - preme - ly kind.

Fill our hearts with Thy rich grace; Tune our lips to sing Thy praise.
Let Thy spir - it now im - part Full sal - va - tion to each heart.
Heal the sick; the cap - tive free: Let us all re - joice in Thee.

1. Our heav-'nly Fa - ther calls, . . . And Christ in -
2. God pit - ies all my griefs; . . . He par - dons

- vites us near; . . . With both our friend - ship
ev - 'ry day; . . . . Al - might - y to . . . . pro -

shall be sweet, And our com - mun - ion dear. . . . . .
- tect my soul, And wise to guide my way. . . . . .

3 Jesus, my living Head,
   I bless Thy faithful care;
Mine Advocate before the throne,
   And my Forerunner there.

4 Here fix, my roving heart;
   Here wait, my warmest love,
Till the communion be complete
   In nobler scenes above.

23   Within these Walls be Peace.

With - in these walls be peace, Love through our bor - ders found;

In all our lit - tle pal - a - ces, Pros - per - i - ty a-bound.

2 God scorns not humble things;
  Here, though the proud despise,
The children of the King of kings
Are training for the skies.

3 May none, who thus are taught,
  From glory be cast down,
But all, through faith and patience, brought
To an immortal crown.

24   Lord, this Day Thy Children meet.

1. Lord, this day Thy chil - dren meet   In Thy courts with will - ing feet;
2. Not a - lone the day of rest   With Thy wor - ship shall be blest;
3. Help us un - to Thee to pray   Hal - low - ing our hap - py day;

Lord, this Day Thy Children meet.—Concluded.

Un - to Thee this day they raise Grate-ful hearts in hymns of praise.
In our pleas-ure and our glee, Lord, we would re - mem - ber Thee.
From Thy pres-ence thus to win Hearts all pure and free from sin.

4 All our pleasures here below,
Saviour, from Thy mercy flow;
Little Children Thou dost love;
Draw our hearts to Thee above.

5 Make, O Lord, our childhood shine
With all lowly grace like Thine !
Then through all eternity
We shall live in heaven with Thee.

25   Jesus, we Thy Promise claim.

1. Je-sus, we Thy prom-ise claim. We are gath - ered in Thy name:

In the midst do Thou ap-pear. Man - i - fest Thy pres - ence here.

2 Sanctify us, Lord, and bless;
Breathe Thy Spirit, give Thy peace;
Come and dwell within each heart,
Light, and life, and joy impart.

3 Make us all in Thee complete.
Make us all for glory meet:
Meet to stand in Thy pure sight,
Partners with the saints in light.

33

26   Heavenly Father, send Thy Blessing.

1. Heavenly Fa-ther, send Thy bless-ing On Thy chil-dren gath-ered here;
2. Bear Thy lambs when they are wea - ry In Thine arms and at Thy breast;

May they all, Thy name con -fess - ing, Be to Thee for ev - er dear.
Through life's des - ert, dry and drear - y, Bring them to Thy heavenly rest.

Ho - ly Sav - iour, who in meekness Didst vouchsafe a Child to be,
Spread Thy gold - en pin - ions o'er them, Ho - ly Spir - it from a - bove;

Guide their steps, and help their weak-ness, Bless and make them like to Thee.
Guide them, lead them, go be - fore them, Give them peace, and joy, and love.

Jesus Lord, we hail Thee King.

1. Je - sus Lord, we hail Thee King! To Thy name ho - san - nas sing!
2. 'Mid life's ope - ning scenes we stand, Far off lies the pleas - ant land;

Ev - er with Thy days re-turn Thoughts of Thee with - in us burn;
Dan - ger waits where - 'er we go, Lurks on ev - ery hand a foe;

Till we seem Thy voice to hear; Till we know that Thou art near.
Strait and steep the heavenward way; Sav - iour, leave us not to stray.

3 Faithful Shepherd, let us share,
  Day by day Thy tender care;
  In temptation's fearful hour
  Save us from its deadly power;
  Thou for us Thyself didst give,
  Teach us how for Thee to live.

4 Father, be our daily guide;
  Jesus, keep us near Thy side;
  Spirit, while we search the mine
  Opened in the word divine,
  Let the sacred page grow bright,
  Glowing in Thy perfect light.

28   Father, again in Jesus' Name we meet.

1. Fa - ther, a - gain in Je - sus' name we meet, And bow in

pen - i - tence be - neath Thy feet; A - gain to Thee our

fee - ble voi - ces raise, To sue for mer - cy, and to sing Thy praise.

2 Alas! unworthy of Thy boundless love,
   Too oft with careless feet from Thee we rove;
   But now encouraged by Thy voice, we come,
   Returning sinners, to a Father's home.

29   God of Heaven! hear our Singing.

1. God of heav - en! hear our sing - ing; On - ly
2. Let Thy king - dom come, we pray Thee; Let the

lit - tle ones are we; ... Yet a great pe -
world in Thee find rest; ... Let all know Thee

ti - tion bring-ing, Fa - ther, now we come to Thee.
and o - bey Thee, Lov - ing, prais - ing, bless - ing, blest.

3 Let the sweet and joyful story
Of the Saviour's wondrous love
Wake on earth a song of glory
Like the angel's song above.

4 Father, send the glorious hour,
Every heart be Thine alone;
For the kingdom and the power
And the glory are Thine own.

37

30   Lord, what Offering shall we bring.

1. Lord, what of-fering shall we bring, At Thine al-tars when we bow?
2. Will-ing hands to lead the blind, Bind the wound-ed, feed the poor;

Hearts, the pure, un-sul-lied spring Whence the kind af-fec-tions flow;
Love, em-brac-ing all our kind, Char-i-ty, with lib-eral store:

Soft com-pas-sion's feel-ing soul, By the melt-ing eye ex-pressed;
Teach us, O Thou heav-enly King, Thus to show our grate-ful mind;

Sym-pa-thy, at whose con-trol, Sor-row leaves the wound-ed breast.
Thus the ac-cept-ed of-fering bring, Love to Thee and all man-kind.

38

31 We are little Pilgrims.

1. We are lit - tle pil - grims, We are stran - gers here;

Though this world is pleas - ant, Sin is ev - er near.

2 We've a better country,
  Where there is no sin ;
  Where the sound of sorrow
  Never cometh in.

3 There are joy and singing,
  There white raiment clean;
  There the blessèd Saviour
  Ever may be seen.

4 There the Lord will welcome,
  With extended hand,
  All His little pilgrims
  To that happy land.

5 Teach us, Lord, Thy precepts
  Always to obey;
  Let Thy spirit guide us
  On our heavenly way.

6 So shall we be ready,
  When this life is o'er,
  To enjoy the glories
  Of the heavenly shore.

7 We are little pilgrims,
  We are strangers here;
  But our home in heaven
  Cometh ever near.

39

1. Now the shades of night are gone; Now the morn-ing light is come;

Lord, may we be Thine to-day; Drive the shades of sin a-way.

2 Fill our souls with heavenly light;
Banish doubt and clear our sight;
In Thy service, Lord, to-day,
May we labor, watch and pray.

3 Keep our haughty passions bound;
Save us from our foes around;
Going out and coming in,
Keep us safe from every sin.

4 When our work of life is past,
Oh, receive us then at last;
Night and sin will be no more,
When we reach the heavenly shore.

33   Jesus, when a little Child.

1. Je - sus, when a lit - tle child, Taught us what we ought to be;
2. As in age and strength He grew, Heav - enly wis - dom filled His breast;

Ho - ly, harm - less, un - de - filed Was the Sav - iour's in - fan - cy;
Crowds at - ten - tive round Him drew, Wondering at their in - fant guest;

All the Fa - ther's glo - ry shone In the per - son of His Son.
Gazed up - on His love - ly face, Saw Him full of truth and grace.

3 In His heavenly Father's house
Jesus spent His early days ;
There He paid His solemn vows,
There proclaimed His Father's praise ;
Thus it was His lot to gain
Favor both with God and man.

4 Father, guide our steps aright
In the way that Jesus trod ;
May it be our great delight
To obey Thy will, O God !
Then to us shall soon be given
Endless bliss with Christ in Heaven.

There's a Friend for little Children.

1. There's a Friend for lit - tle chil - dren, A - bove the bright blue sky,
A Friend who nev - er chang - es, Whose love will nev - er die:
Un - like our friends by na - ture, Who change with chang-ing years,
This Friend is al - ways wor - thy Of that dear name He bears.

2 There's a Home for little children,
  Above the bright blue sky,
Where Jesus reigns in glory,
  A home of peace and joy;
No home on earth is like it,
  Nor can with it compare:
For every one is happy,
  Nor could be happier there.

3 There's a song for little children,
  Above the bright blue sky,
A song that will not weary,
  Though sung continually;
A song which even angels
  Can never, never sing;
They know not Christ as Saviour.
  But worship Him as King.

The Morning bright.

1. The morn - ing bright, With ro - sy light, Has wak'd me from my sleep;

Fa-ther, I own, Thy love a - lone, Thy lit - tle one doth keep.

2 All through the day,
  I humbly pray,
Be Thou my guard and guide ;
  My sins forgive,
  And let me live,
Blest Jesus, near Thy side.

3 Oh, make Thy rest
  Within my breast,
Great Spirit of all grace ;
  Make me like Thee ;
  Then shall I be
Prepared to see Thy face.

We come to Thee, sweet Saviour.

SOLO.

1. We come to Thee, sweet Sav - iour; Just because we need Thee so:
2. We come to Thee, sweet Sav - iour! It is love that makes us come:
3. We come to Thee, sweet Sav - iour! For to whom, Lord! can we go?

None need Thee more than we ... do: Nor are half so vile or low.
We are cer - tain of our wel - come. Of our Fa - ther's wel-come home.
The words of life e - ter - - nal From Thy lips for ev - er flow.

CHORUS.

O boun - ti - ful sal - va - - tion! O life e - ter - nal won! O

We come to Thee, sweet Saviour.—Concluded.

plen - ti - ful   re - demp - tion!   O Blood of   God's dear Son.

4 We come to Thee, sweet Saviour!
  'Tis in answer to Thy call,
Dear hope of the unworthy!
  Dearest merit of us all.—CHO.

5. We come to Thee, sweet Saviour!
  And Thou wilt not ask us why:
We cannot live without Thee,
  And still less without Thee die.—CHO.

37 He knoweth all His Flock full well.

1. He know-eth all His flock full well,   He call-eth them by name;
2. Yes, Je - sus loves His lit - tle lambs; Though small and weak of limb
3. Their help-less-ness is their de-fence, While in His strength they trust;

He loves them ve - ry ten - der-ly,   And al - ways just the same.
They yet are safe, and shall be safe While they keep close to Him.
He know-eth well their fee - ble frames. He know - eth they are dust.

4 And I can be His little lamb,
  Forever I can rest
Gently within the Shepherd's arms
  Upon the Shepherd's breast.

5 Oh, while I live, with hand of faith.
  My blessed Lord I'll hold:
And, gentle Shepherd, when I die.
  Receive me to Thy fold.

45

Hushed was the Evening Hymn.

1. Hushed was the eve - ning hymn, The tem - ple courts were dark;

The lamp was burn - ing dim Be - fore the sa - cred ark;

When sud - den - ly a Voice di - vine Rang thro' the si - lence of the shrine.

2 The old man meek and mild,
   The priest of Israel, slept;
His watch the temple-child,
   The little Levite kept;
And what from Eli's sense was sealed,
The Lord to Hannah's son revealed,

3 Oh, give me Samuel's ear,
   The open ear, O Lord,
Alive and quick to hear
   Each whisper of Thy word;
Like him to answer to Thy call.
And to obey Thee first of all.

4 Oh, give me Samuel's heart,
   A lowly heart, that waits
Where in Thy house Thou art,
   Or watches at Thy gates,
By day and night, a heart that still
Moves at the breathing of Thy will.

5 Oh, give me Samuel's mind,
   A sweet unmurmuring faith,
Obedient and resigned
   To Thee in life and death,
That I may read with childlike eyes
Truths that are hidden from the wise.

Saviour, like a Shepherd lead us.

1. Sav - iour, like a shepherd lead us, Much we need Thy ten - der care;
2. We are Thine, do Thou befriend us, Be the Guar - dian of our way;

In Thy pleas-ant pas-tures feed us, For our use Thy fold pre - pare;
Keep Thy flock, from sin de - fend us, Seek us when we go a - stray;

Bless-ed Je - sus, Bless - ed Je - sus, Thou hast brought us, Thine we are.
Bless-ed Je - sus, Bless - ed Je - sus, Hear the chil - dren when they pray.

3 Thou hast promised to receive us,
   Poor and sinful though we be;
   Thou hast mercy to relieve us,
   Grace to cleanse, and power to free;
   Blessed Jesus,
   Let us early turn to Thee.

4 Early let us seek Thy favor,
   Early let us do Thy will;
   Holy Lord, our only Saviour,
   With Thy grace our bosoms fill:
   Blessed Jesus,
   Thou hast loved us, love us still.

47

40   Jesus, meek and gentle.

dim.

1. Je - sus, meek and gen - tle,   Son   of God most high......
2. Par - don our of - fen - ces,   Loose our cap - tive chains......
3. Give us ho - ly free - dom,   Fill our hearts with love: .....

Pit - ying, lov - ing Sav - iour.   Hear Thy chil-dren's cry.
Break down ev - ery i - - dol   Which our soul de - tains.
Draw us, Ho - ly Je - - sus,   To the realms a - bove.

4 Lead us on our journey,
   Be Thyself the Way,
Through terrestrial darkness,
   To celestial day.

5 Jesus, meek and gentle,
   Son of God most high,
Pitying, loving Saviour,
   Hear Thy children's cry.

41   Jesus a Child His Course begun.

1. Je - sus a child His course be-gun; How radiant dawn'd His heav'nly day!
2. His Fa-ther's business was His care; Yet in man's fa - vor still He grew:

Jesus a Child His Course begun.—Concluded.

And those who such a race would run, As ear-ly should be on their way.
Oh, might we learn by thought and pray'r, Like Him a work of love to do.

3 O children, ask Him to impart
   That spirit clear, that temper mild,
   Which made the mother in her heart
   Keep all the sayings of her child.

4 Bless Him who said, of such as you
   His Father's kingdom is; and still,
   His yoke to bear, His work to do,
   Study His life to learn His will.

42   Ever would I fain be reading.

1. Ev - er would I fain be read - ing In the an-cient Ho - ly Book,
2. How when children came, He blessed them, Suf-fered no man to re-prove;
3. How to all the sick and tear - ful Help was ev - er glad - ly shown;

Of my Sa-viour's gen - tle plead-ing, Truth in ev - ery word and look.
Took them in His arms and press'd them To His heart with words of love.
How He sought the poor and fear - ful, Called them broth-ers and His own.

4 How no contrite soul e'er sought him,
   And was bidden to depart;
   How with gentle words He taught Him,
   Took the death from out his heart.

5 Let me kneel, my Lord, before Thee,
   Let my heart in tears o'erflow;
   Melted by Thy love, adore Thee;
   Blest in Thee, 'mid joy or woe.

43   Dear Jesus, ever at my Side.

1. Dear Je - sus, ev - er at my side, How lov - ing must Thou be,
2. Thy beau - ti - ful and shin - ing face I see not, tho' so near:

To leave Thy home in heav'n to guard A lit - tle child like me!
The sweet-ness of Thy soft, low voice I am too deaf to hear.

3 I cannot feel Thee touch my hand,
   With pressure light and mild,
To check me as my mother did
   When I was but a child;

4 But I have felt Thee in my thought,
   Fighting with sin for me :
And when my heart loves God, I know
   The sweetness is from Thee.

5 And when, dear Saviour, I kneel down,
   Morning and night to prayer,
Something there is within my heart
   Which tells me Thou art there.

6 Yes, when I pray, Thou prayest too,
   The prayer is all for me ;
But when I sleep, Thou sleepest not,
   But watchest patiently.

44   Jesus, holy, undefiled.

1. Je - sus, ho - ly, un - de - filed, Lis - ten to a lit - tle child;
2. Thou hast sent the sun to shine O'er this glo - rious world of Thine;

Jesus, holy, undefiled.—Concluded.

Thou hast sent the glo - rious light, Chas - ing far the si - lent night.
Warmth to give, and pleas - ant glow On each ten - der flow'r be - low.

3 Now the little birds arise,
  Chirping gayly in the skies ;
  Thee, their tiny voices praise
  In the early songs they raise.

4 Thou by whom the birds are fed,
  Give to me my daily bread ;
  And Thy Holy Spirit give,
  Without whom I cannot live.

5 Make me, Lord, obedient, mild,
  As becomes a little child :
  All day long, in every way,
  Teach me what to do or say.

6 Make me, Lord, in work and play
  Thine more truly every day;
  And when Thou at last shalt come,
  Take me to Thy heavenly home.

45   See the shining dew-drops.

1. See the shin - ing dew - drops On the flow - erets strewed,
2. See the morn - ing sun - beams Light - ing up the wood,

Prov - ing as they spar - kle, "God is ev - er good."
Si - lent - ly pro - claim - ing, "God is ev - er good."

3 Hear the mountain streamlet
    In the solitude,
  With its ripple saying,
    " God is ever good."

4 In the leafy tree-tops,
    Where no fears intrude,
  Joyous birds are singing,
    " God is ever good."

Jesus Christ our Saviour.

1. Je - sus Christ our Sav - iour, Once for us a child, In Thy whole be -
- hav - ior Meek, o - be - dient, mild; In Thy foot - steps tread - ing,
We Thy lambs will be, Foe nor danger dread - ing, While we fol - low Thee.

2 For all Thou bestowest,
   All Thou dost withhold ;
Whatsoe'er Thou knowest
   Best for us, Thy fold:
For all gifts and graces
   While we live below,
Till in heavenly places
   We Thy face shall know.

3 Let Thine angels guide us :
   Let Thine arms enfold ;
In Thy bosom hide us,
   Sheltered from the cold:
To Thyself us gather,
   'Mid the ransomed host,
Praising Thee, the Father
   And the Holy Ghost.

47   Saviour, Who Thy Flock art feeding.

1. Sav - iour, Who Thy flock art feed - ing, With the shep-herd's kind-est care,
2. Nev - er, from Thy past - ure rov - ing, Let them be the li - on's prey;

Org. ped.

All   the fee - ble gent - ly lead - ing, While the lambs Thy bo - som share;
Let   Thy ten - der - ness so lov - ing Keep them all life's dangerous way;

Now these lit - tle ones re - ceiv - ing, Fold them in Thy gra - cious arm;
Then, with - in Thy fold e - ter - nal, Let them find a rest - ing place;

There, we know, Thy word be - liev - ing, On - ly there, se - cure from harm.
Feed in pas - tures ev - er ver - nal, Drink the riv - ers of Thy grace.

48   Jesus, Lord and Saviour.

1. Je - sus, Lord and Sav - iour! God of might and pow'r!
2. Na - ture can - not hold Thee, Heav'n is all too strait

Thou Thy - self art dwell - ing In Thy saints this hour.
For Thine end - less glo - ry, And Thy roy - al state.

3 Out beyond the shining
  Of the farthest star.
Thou art ever stretching
  Infinitely far.

4 Yet the hearts of children
  Hold what worlds cannot,
And the God of wonders
  Loves the lowly spot.

5 Jesus, Lord and Saviour!
  Be Thou in us now;
Fill us with Thy goodness,
  Till our hearts o'erflow.

6 Multiply our graces,
  Chiefly love and fear,
And, dear Lord! the chiefest,
  Grace to persevere.

49   O Jesus! God and Man!

1. O Je - sus! God and Man! For love of chil-dren once a child!

O Jesus! God and Man!—Concluded.

O Je - sus! God and Man! We hail Thee Sav - iour sweet and mild.

2 O Jesus! God and Man!
   Make us poor children dear to Thee,
   And lead us to Thyself,
   To love Thee for eternity.

3 O Jesus! God's dear Son!
   On Thee for grace we children call:
   Make us all men to love,
   But to love Thee beyond them all.

4 O Jesus! bless our work,
   Our sorrows soothe, our sins forgive;
   O happy, happy they
   Who in the Church of Jesus live!

5 O God, most great and good,
   At work or play, by night or day,
   Make us remember Thee,
   Who so rememberest us alway.

50 All Things bright and beautiful.

1. All things bright and beau-ti - ful, All crea-tures great and small,
2. Each lit - tle flow'r that o - pens, Each lit - tle bird that sings,

All things wise and won-der - ful, The Lord God made them all.
He made their glow-ing col - ors He made their ti - ny wings.

3 The purple-headed mountain,
   The river running by,
   The morning and the sunset,
   That lighteth up the sky.

4 The tall trees in the greenwood,
   The pleasant summer sun,
   The ripe fruits in the garden,
   He made them every one.

Gracious Saviour, holy Shepherd!

1. Gra-cious Sav-iour, ho - ly Shepherd, Lit-tle ones are dear to Thee:
2. Ten - der Shep-herd, nev - er leave them From Thy fold to go a-stray;
3. Let Thy ho - ly word instruct them; Fill their minds with heavenly light;
4. Taught to lisp Thy ho - ly prais-es, Which on earth Thy chil-dren sing,

Gath-ered with Thine arms, and car-ried In Thy bos - om, may they be.
By Thy warn-ing love di - rect-ed, May they walk the nar-row way;
Let Thy love and grace constrain them To ap - prove what - e'er is right;
With both lips and hearts un-feign-èd Glad thank - of - ferings may they bring;

Sweet - ly, fond - ly, safe - ly tend-ed, From all want and dan - ger free.
Thus di - rect them, thus de-fend them, Lest they fall an ea - sy prey.
Let them feel Thy yoke is ea - sy, Let them prove Thy bur - den light.
Then with all Thy saints in glo - ry, Join to praise their Lord and King.

Jesus the Shepherd of the Sheep.

1. Je - sus the Shep - herd of the sheep, Thy lit - tle flock in safe - ty keep,
2. Se-cure them from the scorching beam, And lead them to the liv - ing stream;

The flock for which Thou cam'st from heav'n, The flock for which Thy life was given.
In ver - dant pas - tures let them lie, And watch them with a shepherd's eye!

Oh guard Thy sheep from beasts of prey, And guide them that they nev - er stray;
Oh may Thy sheep dis - cern Thy voice, And in its sa - cred sound re - joice;

Cher - ish the young, sus - tain the old, Let none be fee - ble in Thy fold.
From strangers may they ev - er flee, And know no oth - er guide but Thee.

1. { Je - sus. gen - tlest Sav - iour!   God   of   might and   pow'r!
   { Out   be - yond the   shin - ing   Of   the   far - thest   star,

2. { Je - sus,   gen - tlest Sav - iour!   Thou   art   in   us   now:
   { Mul - ti - ply   our   gra - ces,   Chief - ly   love   and   fear,

FINE.

Thou Thy - self   art   dwell - ing   In   us   at   this   hour. }
Thou   art   ev - er   stretch - ing   In - fi - nite - ly   far. }
Fill   us   full   of   good - ness,   Till   our hearts o'er - flow. }
And,   dear Lord! the   chief - est—   Grace   to   per - se - vere. }

Na - ture   can - not hold   Thee,   Heav'n   is   all   too   strait
Pray   the   pray'r with - in . . . us,   That   to heav'n shall   rise;

D.C.

For   Thine end - less   glo - ry.   And Thy roy - al   state.
Sing   the   song   that   an - gels   Sing a - bove the   skies.

58

Songs of Praise the Angels sang.

1. Songs of praise the an-gels sang, Heaven with hal-le-lu-jahs rang,

When Je-ho-vah's work be-gun, When He spake and it was done.

2 Songs of praise awoke the morn,
   When the Prince of Peace was born;
   Songs of praise arose when He
   Captive led captivity.

3 Saints below, with heart and voice,
   Still in songs of praise rejoice;
   Learning here, by faith and love,
   Songs of praise to sing above.

55   Holy, Holy, Holy! Lord God Almighty.

1. Ho-ly, ho-ly, ho-ly! Lord God Al-migh-ty! Grate-ful-ly a-dor-ing, Our song shall rise to Thee. Ho-ly, ho-ly, ho-ly, Mer-ci-ful and Migh-ty, God in Three Per-sons, Blessed Trin-i-ty!

2 Holy, holy, holy! all the saints adore Thee,
  Casting down their golden crowns around the glassy sea;
  Cherubim and seraphim falling down before Thee,
  Who wert, and art, and evermore shalt be.

3 Holy, holy, holy! though the darkness hide Thee,
  Though the eye of sinful man Thy glory may not see;
  Only Thou art holy; there is none beside Thee
  Perfect in power, in love and purity.

Worship, Honor, Glory, Blessing.

1. Wor-ship, hon-or, glo-ry, bless-ing, Lord, we of-fer to Thy name:

Young and old, their praise ex-press-ing, Join Thy good-ness to pro-claim.

As the saints in heaven a-dore Thee, We would bow be-fore Thy throne:

As the an-gels serve be-fore Thee, So on earth Thy will be done.

57   Praise, my Soul, the King of Heaven.

1. Praise, my soul, the King of Heav-en, To His feet thy tri-bute bring;

Ransomed, heal'd, re-stored, for-giv-en, Ev-er-more His prais-es sing:

Hal-le-lu-jah! hal-le-lu-jah! Praise the ev-er-last-ing King.

2 Father-like, He tends and spares us,
    Well our feeble frame He knows;
    In His hands He gently bears us,
    Rescues us from all our foes;
    Hallelujah! hallelujah!
    Widely yet His mercy flows.

3 Angels in the height adore Him,
    Ye behold Him face to face;
    Saints triumphant bow before Him,
    Gathered in from every race,
    Hallelujah! hallelujah!
    Praise with us the God of grace.

Come, Thou Almighty King.

1. Come, Thou al - migh - ty King, Help us Thy name to sing,

Help us to praise; Fa - ther all glo - ri - ous, O'er all vic -

- to - ri - ous, Come and reign ov - er us, An - cient of days.

2 Come, Thou incarnate Word
Gird on Thy mighty sword;
  Our prayer attend;
Come, and Thy people bless,
And give Thy word success;
Spirit of holiness,
  On us descend.

3 Come, holy Comforter,
Thy sacred witness bear,
  In this glad hour.
Thou, who almighty art,
Now rule in every heart,
And ne'er from us depart,
  Spirit of power.

63

1. Let us with a glad-some mind, Praise the Lord. for He is kind:

For His mer - cies shall en - dure, Ev - er faith-ful ev - er sure.

He, with all com-mand - ing might, Filled the new-made world with light:

For His mer - cies shall en - dure, Ev - er faith - ful, ev - er sure.

2 All things living He doth feed:
His full hand supplies their need;
For His mercies shall endure,
Ever faithful, ever sure.
He His chosen race did bless.
In the wasteful wilderness:
For His mercies shall endure.
Ever faithful. ever sure.

3 He hath, with a piteous eye.
Looked upon our misery:
For His mercies shall endure.
Ever faithful, ever sure.
Let us, then. with gladsome mind.
Praise the Lord. for He is kind:
For His mercies shall endure,
Ever faithful. ever sure.

60   Day by Day we magnify Thee.

Unison.

1. { Day by day we mag - ni - fy Thee,—When our hymns in school we raise. }
  { Dai - ly work be - gun and end - ed, With the dai - ly voice of praise. }

2. { Day by day we mag - ni - fy Thee,—When for Je - sus' sake we try. }
  { Ev - ery wrong to bear with patience, Ev - ery sin to mor - ti - fy. }

In Parts.

1. Day by day we mag - ni - fy Thee,—Not in words of praise a - lone;
2. Day by day we mag - ni - fy Thee, Till our days on earth shall cease,

Unison.

1. Truth - ful lips and meek o - be - dience, Show Thy glo - ry in Thine own.
2. Till we rest from these our la - bors. Wait - ing for Thy day in peace.

65

61   Praise the Lord, ye Heavens, adore Him.

1. Praise the Lord, ye heavens, a-dore Him, Praise Him, an-gels, in the height;
2. Praise the Lord, for He is glo-rious; Nev - er shall His prom-ise fail;

Sun and moon, re - joice be - fore Him; Praise Him, all ye stars of light.
God hath made His saints vic - to - rious, Sin and death shall not pre - vail.

Praise the Lord, for He hath spok - en; Worlds His might - y voice o - beyed;
Praise the God of our sal - va - tion, Hosts on high His power pro-claim;

Laws, that nev - er shall be brok - en, For their guidance He hath made.
Heaven and earth and all cre - a - tion Laud and mag - ni - fy His name.

Angel Voices, ever singing.

1. An - gel voi - ces, ev - er sing - ing Round Thy throne of light—

An - gel harps for ev - er ring - ing, Rest not day nor night;

Thousands on - ly live to bless Thee, And con - fess Thee, Lord of might.

2 Thou, who art beyond the farthest,
   Mortal eye can scan;
Can it be that Thou regardest
   Songs of sinful man?
Can we know that Thou art near us,
   And wilt hear us?
      Yea, we can.

3 Here, great God, to-day we offer
   Of Thine own to Thee;
And for Thine acceptance proffer,
   All unworthily,
Hearts and minds, and hands and voices,
   In our choicest
      Melody.

63   Heavenly Father, sovereign Lord.

1. Heav-enly Fa - ther, sovereign Lord, Be Thy glo-rious name a - dored!
2. Tho' un - wor - thy, Lord, Thine ear; Deign our hum - ble songs to hear:

Lord, Thy mer-cies nev - er fail; Hail ce - les - tial good-ness hail!
Pur - er praise we hope to bring, When a - round Thy throne we sing.

3 While on earth ordained to stay,
Guide our footsteps in Thy way,
Till we come to dwell with Thee,
Till we all Thy glory see.

4 Then with angel-harps again,
We will wake a nobler strain:
There, in joyful songs of praise,
Our triumphant voices raise.

64   God is Love; His Mercy brightens.

1. God is love; His mer - cy bright-ens All the path in which we rove:

God is Love; His Mercy brightens.—Concluded.

Bliss He wakes, and woe He light-ens; God is wis - dom, God is love.

2 E'en the hour that darkest seemeth,
  Will His changeless goodness prove ;
  From the gloom His brightness streameth ;
  God is wisdom, God is love.

3 He with earthly cares entwineth
  Hope and comfort from above ;
  Everywhere His glory shineth ;
  God is wisdom, God is love.

65   All ye Nations, praise the Lord!

1. All ye na - tions, praise the Lord, All ye lands, your voic-es raise;

Heav'n and earth, with loud ac - cord, Praise the Lord, for - ev - er praise.

2 For His truth and mercy stand,
  Past, and present, and to be ;
  Like the years of His right hand,
  Like His own eternity.

3 Praise Him, ye who know His love ;
  Praise Him from the depths beneath ;
  Praise Him in the heights above :
  Praise your Maker, all that breathe.

1. Up-ward where the stars are burn-ing. Si - lent, si - lent   in   their turning,
2. Far   beyond that arch of glad-ness. Far beyond these clouds of sad-ness.

Round the nev - er - chang-ing pole: Up - ward where the sky is brightest.
Are the man - y man-sions fair. Far from pain and sin and fol - ly.

ri - ten - u - to.

Upward where the blue is lightest. Lift I now my long-ing soul. . . . . .
In that pal - ace of the ho - ly.   I would find my man-sion there. . . . . .

In heavenly Love abiding.

1. In heavenly love a - bid - ing, No change my heart shall fear; And safe is such con-
- fid - ing, For noth - ing chang-es here. The storm may roar with - out me,
My heart may low be laid; But God is round a - bout me, And can I be dismayed?

2 Wherever He may guide me,
   No want shall turn me back :
 My Shepherd is beside me,
   And nothing can I lack.
 His wisdom ever waketh;
   His sight is never dim:
 He knows the way He taketh,
   And I will walk with Him.

3 Green pastures are before me,
   Which yet I have not seen;
 Bright skies will soon be o'er me,
   Where the dark clouds have been.
 My hope I cannot measure :
   My path to life is free :
 My Saviour has my treasure,
   And He will walk with me.

71

68   Father, hear the Prayer we offer!

1. Fa - ther hear the prayer we of - fer! Not for ease our prayer shall be,
2. Not for ev - er in green pas - tures Do we ask our way to be;

But for strength, that we may ev - er Live our lives cour-age - ous - ly.
But by steep and rug - ged path - ways Would we strive to climb to Thee.

3 Not for ever in still waters
   Would we ask that we may stay,
   But would win the living fountains
   From the rocks along our way.

Copyright, 1886, by Cong'l S. S. and Pub. Soc.

4 Be our strength in hours of weakness;
   In our wanderings be our guide;
   Through endeavor, failure, danger,
   Father! be Thou at our side.

69   Holy, holy, holy Lord!

1. Ho - ly, ho - ly, ho - ly Lord! Be Thy glo - rious name a - dored;

Holy, holy, holy Lord!—Concluded.

Lord! Thy mer - cies nev - er fail; Hail, ce - les - tial good - ness, hail!

2 Though unworthy, Lord, Thine ear,
Deign our humble songs to hear;
Purer praise we hope to bring,
When around Thy throne we sing.

3 Lord! Thy mercies never fail;
Hail, celestial goodness, hail!
Holy, holy, holy Lord!
Be Thy glorious name adored.

70 Around the Throne of God a Band.

1. Around the throne of God a band Of glo - rious an - gels ev - er stand;
2. Some wait around Him, read - y still To sing His praise and do His will;

Bright things they see, sweet harps they hold, And on their heads are crowns of gold.
And some, when He commands them, go To guard His ser - vants here be - low.

3 Lord, give Thy angels every day
Command to guide us on our way;
And bid them every evening keep
Their watch around us while we sleep.

4 So shall no wicked thing draw near
To do us harm or cause us fear:
And we shall dwell, when life is past,
With angels round Thy throne at last.

71   Love divine, all Love excelling.

1. Love di-vine, all love ex-cel-ling. Joy of heaven, to earth come down:

Fix in us Thy hum-ble dwell-ing; All Thy faith-ful mer-cies crown.

Je-sus, Thou art all com-pas-sion; Pure, un-bound-ed love Thou art:

Vis-it us with Thy sal-va-tion: En-ter ev-ery long-ing heart.

74

Love divine, all Love excelling.—Concluded.

2 Come, almighty to deliver,
　　Let us all Thy grace receive ;
　Suddenly return, and never,
　　Never more Thy temples leave.
　Thee we would be always blessing,
　　Serve Thee as Thy hosts above ;
　Pray and praise Thee without ceasing;
　　Glory in Thy precious love.

3 Finish, then, Thy new creation;
　　Pure, unspotted may we be :
　Let us see our whole salvation
　　Perfectly secured in Thee ;
　Changed from glory into glory,
　　Till in heaven we take our place ;
　Till we cast our crowns before Thee,
　　Lost in wonder, love and praise.

72　　Lift up to God the Voice of Praise.

1. Lift up to God the voice of praise, Whose breath our souls in - spired,

Loud and more loud the an -thems raise, With grate-ful ar - dor fired.

2 Lift up to God the voice of praise,
　From whom salvation flows,
　Who sent his Son our souls to save
　From everlasting woes.

3 Lift up to God the voice of praise,
　For hope's transporting ray,
　Which lights through darkest shades of
　To realms of endless day.　　[death,

75

73   Breathe on me, Breath of God.

1. Breathe on me. Breath of God, Fill me with life a - new.
2. Breathe on me, Breath of God, Un - til my heart is pure,

That I may love what Thou dost love, And do what Thou wouldst do.
Un - til with Thee I will one will, To do or to en - dure.

3 Breathe on me, Breath of God,
    Till I am wholly Thine,
    Till all this earthly part of me
    Glows with Thy fire divine.

4 Breathe on me, Breath of God,
    So shall I never die,
    But live with Thee the perfect life
    Of Thine eternity.

74   Thy Home is with the Humble, Lord.

1. Thy home is with the hum-ble, Lord, Thou lov'st the sim - ple best:

Thy Home is with the Humble, Lord.—Concluded.

Thy lodg-ing is in child-like hearts; Thou mak-est there Thy rest.

2 Dear Comforter! Eternal love !
If Thou wilt stay with me,
Of lowly thoughts and simple ways,
I'll build a house for Thee.

3 Who made this beating heart of mine.
But Thou, my heavenly Guest?
Let none possess it, Lord, but Thee,
And let it be Thy rest.

75   Holy Father, heavenly King.

1. Ho-ly Fa-ther, heavenly King. O'er me spread Thy guar-dian wing:

When by trembling fears distressed, Let me flee to Thee and rest.

2 Call me, keep me by Thy side.
Teach me there alone to hide :
Where for safety should I flee,
If my footsteps strayed from Thee?

3 Warn me with Thy gentle voice:
Point my path, and guide my choice ;
Let me, Lord, in Thee possess
Wisdom, peace and righteousness.

Lead us, heavenly Father, lead us.

1. Lead us, heavenly Fa - ther, lead us O'er the world's tem-pestuous sea;

Guard us, guide us, keep us, feed us, For we have no help but Thee;

Yet pos - sess - ing Ev - ery bless-ing, If our God our Fa - ther be.

2 Saviour, breath forgivness o'er us;
   All our weakness Thou dost know;
   Thou didst tread this earth before us;
   Thou didst feel its keenest woe;
       Lone and dreary,
       Faint and weary,
   Through the desert Thou didst go.

3 Spirit of our God, descending,
   Fill our hearts with heavenly joy;
   Love with every passion blending,
   Pleasure that can never cloy;
       Thus provided,
       Pardoned, guided,
   Nothing can our peace destroy.

77　　　O Jesus, King most wonderful.

1. O Je - sus, King most won - der - ful, Thou Con - quer - or re - nowned;

Thou sweetness most in - ef - fa - ble, In whom all joys are found.

2 When once Thou visitest the heart,
　　Then truth begins to shine,
　Then earthly vanities depart,
　　Then kindles love divine.

3 Thee may our tongues for ever bless;
　　Thee, may we love alone;
　And ever in our lives express
　　The image of Thine own.

78 — Hail to the Lord's Anointed.

1. { Hail to the Lord's An - oint - ed, Great Da - vid's great - er Son! }
   { Hail in the time ap - point - ed, His reign on earth be - gun! }
2. { He shall come down like show - ers Up - on the fruit - ful earth, }
   { And joy and hope like flow - ers, Spring in His path to birth: }

He comes to break op - pres - sion, To set the cap - tive free,
Be - fore Him on the moun - tains Shall peace, the her - ald, go;

To take a - way trans - gres - sion, And rule in eq - ui - ty.
And from a thous-and foun - tains Shall grace un - ceas - ing flow.

3 Kings shall fall down before Him,
    And gold and incense bring:
All nations shall adore Him,
    His praise all people sing;
For Him shall prayer unceasing
    And daily vows ascend;
His kingdom still increasing,
    A kingdom without end.

4 O'er every foe victorious,
    He on His throne shall rest;
From age to age more glorious,
    All blessing and all blest;
The tide of time shall never
    His covenant remove;
His Name shall stand for ever,
    That name to us is Love.

79 When shall the Voice of Singing.

1. When shall the voice of sing - ing Flow joy - ful - ly a - long?
2. Then from the crag - gy moun - tains The sa - cred shout shall fly,

When hill and val - ley ring - ing With one tri - um - phant song,
And sha - dy vales and foun - tains Shall ech - o the re - ply;

Pro-claim the con - test end - ed, And Him who once was slain,
High tower and low - ly dwell - ing Shall send the cho - rus round,

A - gain to earth de - scend - ed, In right-eous - ness to reign.
All hal - le - lu - jahs swell - ing In one e - ter - nal sound.

81

Hark! the Sound of holy Voices.

1. Hark! the sound of ho - ly voic - es Chant-ing, at the crys - tal sea,

Hal - le - lu - jah! Hal - le - lu - jah! Hal - le - lu - jah! Lord, to Thee;

Mul - ti - tude which none can num - ber, Like the stars in glo - ry stands,

Clothed in white ap - par - el, hold - ing Palms of vic-tory in their hands.

2 Patriarch and holy Prophet,
　Who prepared the way of Christ,
King. Apostle, Saint, Confessor,
　Martyr and Evangelist.
Saintly Maiden. goodly Matron,
　Widows who have watched to prayer,
Joined in holy concert. singing
　To the Lord of all, are there.

3 Marching with Thy Cross their banner,
　They have triumphed following
Thee, the Captain of salvation,
　Thee their Saviour and their King;
Gladly, Lord, with Thee they suffered;
　Gladly, Lord, with Thee they died;
And by death to life immortal
　They were born and glorified.

At the Name of Jesus.

1. At the name of Je - sus Ev - ery knee shall bow,

Ev - ery tongue con - fess Him King of glo - ry now:

'Tis the Fa-ther's pleas - ure We should call Him Lord, . . .

Who from the be - gin - - ning Was the migh - ty word.

2 In your hearts enthrone Him;
    There let Him subdue
All that is not holy.
    All that is not true;
Crown Him as your Captain
    In temptation's hour;
Let His will enfold you
    In its light and power.

3 Brothers, this Lord Jesus
    Shall return again,
With His Father's glory,
    With His angel train;
For all wreaths of empire,
    Meet upon His brow,
And our hearts confess Him
    King of glory now.

Crown Him with many Crowns.

1. Crown Him with man - y crowns, The Lamb up - on His throne;

Hark! how the heav - enly an - them drowns All mu - sic but its own.

A - wake my soul, and sing Of Him who died for thee,

And hail Him as thy glo - rious King, Thro' all e - ter - ni - ty.

2 Crown Him the Lord of Life!
  Who triumphed o'er the grave,
And rose victorious in the strife
  For those He came to save;
His glories now we sing,
  Who died, and rose on high;
Who died, eternal life to bring,
  And lives that death may die.

3 Crown Him of lords the Lord,
  Who over all doth reign,
Who once on earth, the Incarnate Word,
  For ransomed sinners slain,
Now lives in realms of light,
  Where saints with angels sing
Their songs before Him day and night,
  Their God, Redeemer, King.

Fairest Lord Jesus!

1. Fair - est Lord Je - sus! Ru - ler of all na - ture! O Thou of God and man the Son! Thee will I cher - ish, Thee will I hon - or, Thou! my soul's glo - ry, joy and crown.

2 Fair are the meadows,
　　Fairer still the woodlands,
Robed in the blooming garb of spring;
　　Jesus is fairer,
　　Jesus is purer,
Who makes the woful heart to sing.

3 Fair is the sunshine,
　　Fairer still the moonlight,
And all the twinkling starry host;
　　Jesus shines brighter,
　　Jesus shines purer,
Than all the angels heaven can boast.

Hail! Thou once despised Jesus.

1. Hail! Thou once de-spis-ed Je-sus, Hail! Thou Gal-i-le-an King;

Thou didst suf-fer to re-lease us; Thou didst free sal-va-tion bring.

Hail! Thou ag-o-niz-ing Sav-iour, Bear-er of our sin and shame,

By Thy mer-its we find fa-vor; Life is giv-en through Thy name.

2 Jesus, hail! enthroned in glory,
   There for ever to abide ;
All the heavenly hosts adore Thee,
   Seated at Thy Father's side ;
There for sinners Thou art pleading :
   There Thou dost our place prepare ;
Ever for us interceding,
   Till in Glory we appear.

3 Worship, honor, power and blessing,
   Thou art worthy to receive :
Loudest praises, without ceasing,
   Meet it is for us to give :
Help, ye bright angelic spirits,
   Bring your sweetest, noblest lays ;
Help to sing our Saviour's merits,
   Help to chant Immanuel's praise.

Jesus came, the Heavens adoring.

1. Je - sus came, the heavens a - dor - ing, Came with peace from realms on high;

Je - sus came for man's re - demption, Low - ly came on earth to die;

Hal - le - lu - jah! hal - le - lu - jah! Came in deep hu - mil - i - ty.

2 Jesus comes in joy and sorrow,
   Shares alike our hopes and fears;
Jesus comes, whate'er befalls us,
   Glads our hearts and dries our tears;
   Hallelujah ! hallelujah !
   Cheering e'en our failing years.

3 Jesus comes on clouds triumphant,
   When the heavens shall pass away;
Jesus comes again in glory;
   Let us then our homage pay;
   Hallelujah ! ever singing,
   Till the dawn of endless day.

86   Glory be to Jesus.

1. Glo - ry be to Je - sus, Who, in bit - ter pains,
2. Grace and life e - ter - nal, In that blood I find;

Poured for me His life - blood From His sa - cred veins.
Blest be His com - pas - sion In - fi - nite - ly kind.

3 Oft as earth exulting
  Wafts its praise on high,
  Angel-hosts rejoicing,
  Make their glad reply.

4 Lift ye then your voices;
  Swell the mighty flood;
  Louder still and louder
  Praise His precious blood.

87   The King of Love my Shepherd is.

1. The King of love my Shepherd is, Whose good-ness fail - eth nev - er;
2. Where streams of liv - ing wa - ter flow, My ran - somed soul he lead - eth,

The King of Love my Shepherd is.—Concluded.

I noth-ing lack if I am His, And He is mine for ev - er.
And, where the ver-dant pas-tures grow, With food ce-les-tial feed - eth.

3 Perverse and foolish, oft I strayed,
But yet in love He sought me,
And on His shoulder gently laid,
And home, rejoicing, brought me.

4 And so through all the length of days
Thy goodness faileth never;
Good Shepherd, may I sing Thy praise
Within Thy house for ever.

88   O Jesus, Jesus! dearest Lord.

1. O Je-sus, Je-sus! dear-est Lord! For-give me if I say
2. I love Thee so, I know not how My trans-ports to con - trol;

For ver - y love Thy sa - cred name A thou-sand times a day.
Thy love is like a burn-ing fire With-in my ver - y soul.

3 For Thou to me art all in all,
My honor and my wealth;
My heart's desire, my body's strength,
My soul's eternal health.

4 O Jesus, Jesus! sweetest Lord!
What art Thou not to me?
Each hour brings joy before unknown,
Each day new liberty.

89   To Thee, O dear, dear Saviour.

1. To Thee, O dear, dear Sav-iour, My spir-it turns for rest; My peace is in Thy
2. In Thee my trust a - bid - eth, On Thee my hope relies, O Thou whose love pro-

fa - vor, My pil-low on Thy breast; Though all the world de - ceive me,
vid - eth For all be-neath the skies; O Thou whose mer - cy found me,

I know that I am Thine, And Thou wilt nev-er leave me, O blessed Saviour mine.
From bondage set me free, And thus for-ev-er bound me With three-fold cords to Thee.

3 Alas! that I should ever
   Have failed in love to Thee,
The only one who never
   Forgot or slighted me!
Oh, for a heart to love Thee
   More truly as I ought,
And nothing place above Thee
   In deed, or word, or thought.

4 Oh, for that choicest blessing
   Of living in Thy love,
And thus on earth possessing
   The peace of heaven above;
Oh, for the bliss that by it
   The soul securely knows
The holy calm and quiet
   Of faith's serene repose.

I could not do without Thee.

1. I could not do with-out Thee, I can-not stand a - lone,

I have no strength or good - ness, No wis - dom of my own;

But Thou be - lov - ed Sav - iour Art all in all to me,

And per - fect strength in weak - ness Is theirs who lean on Thee.

2 I could not do without Thee,
    For, Oh! the way is long.
  And I am often weary,
    And sigh replaces song.
  How could I do without Thee?
    I do not know the way;
  Thou knowest, and Thou leadest,
    And wilt not let me stray.

3 I could not do without Thee,
    O Jesus, Saviour dear!
  E'en when my eyes are holden,
    I know that Thou art near.
  How dreary and how lonely
    This changeful life would be
  Without the sweet communion,
    The secret rest with Thee.

I need Thee, precious Jesus.

1. I need Thee, pre-cious Je - sus, For I am full of sin;
2. I need Thee, pre-cious Je - sus, For I am ve - ry poor;

My soul is dark and guil - ty, My heart is dead with - in:
A stran - ger and a pil - grim, I have no earth - ly store;

I need the cleans - ing foun - tain Where I can al - ways flee,—
I need the love of Je - sus To cheer me on my way,

The blood of Christ most pre - cious, The sin - ner's per - fect plea.
To guide my doubt - ing foot - steps, To be my strength and stay.

I need Thee, precious Jesus.—Concluded.

3 I need Thee, precious Jesus,
   I need a friend like Thee;
A friend to soothe and pity,
   A friend to care for me.
I need the heart of Jesus,
   To feel each anxious care,
To bear my every burden,
   And all my sorrow share.

4 I need Thee, precious Jesus,
   And hope to see Thee soon,
Encircled with the rainbow,
   And seated on Thy throne;
There, with Thy blood-bought children,
   My joy shall ever be,
To sing Thy praise, Lord Jesus,
   To gaze, my Lord, on Thee.

92   Jesus, Love eternal.

1. Je - sus, love e - ter - nal, Bliss of souls su - per - nal, What a joy must
2. Mind and strong en-deav - or Now are Thine for - ev - er; Mer - ri - ly they

Thou im-part When Thou en-ter - est a heart! When Thou en-ter-est a heart!
leap for glee, They are glad be-cause of Thee, They are glad because of Thee.

3 Lord, no longer leave me,
   Bitterly I grieve me
Waiting here; I would abide
Resting ever at Thy side.

4 All the gifts, Lord Jesus,
   Of Thy hands are precious;
But there's none can ever be
What Thyself, Lord, art to me.

93   O Jesus, Thou the Beauty art.

1. O Je - sus, Thou the beau - ty art Of an - gel - worlds a - bove;
2. O most sweet Je - sus! hear the sighs Which un - to Thee we send;

Thy name is mu - sic to the heart, En-chant-ing it with love.
To Thee our in-most spir - it cries, My be - ing's hope and end.

3 Stay with us, Lord! and with Thy light
  Illume the soul's abyss;
  Scatter the darkness of our night,
  And fill the world with bliss.

4 O Jesus, King of earth and heaven,
  Our love and joy! to Thee
  Be honor, thanks and blessing given
  Through all eternity!

94   Loving Shepherd of Thy Sheep.

1. Lov - ing Shep-herd of Thy sheep, Keep me, Lord, in safe - ty keep,
2. Lov - ing Shep-herd, Thou didst give Thine own life that I might live;

Loving Shepherd of Thy Sheep.—Concluded.

Noth - ing can Thy power with-stand, None can pluck me from Thy hand.
May I love Thee day by day; Glad - ly Thy sweet will o - bey.

3 Loving Shepherd, ever near,
Teach me still Thy voice to hear;
Suffer not my foot to stray
From the strait and narrow way.

4 Where Thou leadest may I go;
Walking in Thy steps below;
Then, before Thy Father's throne,
Jesus, claim me for Thine own.

95   Saviour, Source of every Blessing.

1. Sav - iour, source of ev - ery bless-ing, Tune my heart to grate-ful lays;
2. Teach me some mel - o - dious meas-ure, Sung by rap-tured saints a - bove;

Streams of mer - cy, nev - er ceas - ing, Call for cease-less songs of praise.
Fill my soul with sa - cred pleas - ure, While I sing re-deem - ing love.

3 Thou didst seek me when a stranger,
Wandering from the fold of God;
Thou, to save my soul from danger,
Didst redeem me with Thy blood.

4 By Thy hand restored, defended,
Safe through life, thus far, I'm come;
Safe, O Lord, when life is ended,
Bring me to my heavenly home.

96   My Soul is full of sweet Content.

1. My soul is full of sweet con - tent, My heart is gay and glad;
2. Tho' slight the work I have to do, I do it with good will;

He giv - eth songs the live - long night, And how can I be sad?
Tho' small my sheaves and ver - y few, My place I glad - ly fill.

3 I know the goodness of my God,
    His mercy, grace and peace :
    Great is the love He hath for me,
    His kindness cannot cease.

4 His ways are high and far above
    The blindness of my sight;
    And like the sun in heaven, His love
    Floods all my world with light.

97   My Spirit longs for Thee.

1. My spir - it longs for Thee With - in my trou - bled breast;
2. Of so di - vine a Guest Un-worth - y though I be,

My Spirit longs for Thee.—Concluded.

Though I un - wor - thy be Of so di - vine a Guest.
Yet has my heart no rest Un - less it come from Thee.

3 Unless it come from Thee,
  In vain I look around;
  In all that I can see
  No rest is to be found.

4 No rest is to be found
  But in Thy blessed love :
  Oh, let my wish be crowned,
  And send it from above.

98   In the Cross of Christ I glory.

1. In the cross of Christ I glo - ry; Tow - 'ring o'er the wrecks of time,
2. When the woes of life o'er take me, Hopes de - ceive, and fears an - noy.

All the light of sa - cred sto - ry Gath - ers round its head sub - lime.
Nev - er shall the cross for - sake me; Lo! it glows with peace and joy.

3 When the sun of bliss is beaming
  Light and love upon my way,
  From the cross the radiance streaming,
  Adds more lustre to the day.

4 Bane and blessing, pain and pleasure,
  By the cross are sanctified;
  Peace is there, that knows no measure,
  Joys, that through all time abide.

97

Oh where is He that trod the Sea?

1. Oh, where is He that trod the sea? Oh, where is He that spake,
And de - mons from their vic - tims flee, The dead from slum - ber wake?
The pal - sied rise in free - dom strong, The dumb men talk and sing,
And from blind eyes be - night - ed long, Bright beams of morn - ing spring.

2 Oh, where is He that trod the sea?
My soul! the Lord is here:
Let all thy fears be hushed in thee,
And leap, and look, and hear.
Thy utmost needs He'll satisfy;
Art thou diseased or dumb?
Or dost thou in thy hunger cry?
Behold thy Helper come!

100   We saw Thee not when Thou didst come.

1. We saw Thee not when Thou didst come To this poor world of sin and death,
2. We did not see Thee lift - ed high, A - mid that wild and sav - age crew;

Nor e'er be - held Thy cot - tage home In that des - pis - ed Naz - a - reth;
Nor heard Thy meek, im - plor - ing cry, "For-give, they know not what they do!"

But we be - lieve Thy foot - steps trod Its streets and plains, Thou Son of God.
Yet we be-lieve the deed was done, Which shook the earth and veiled the sun.

3 We stood not by the empty tomb,
Wherein Thy sacred body lay;
Nor sat within that upper room,
Nor met Thee in the open way;
But we believe that angels said,
"Why seek the living with the dead?"

4 And now that Thou dost reign on high,
And thence Thy waiting people bless,
No ray of glory from the sky
Doth shine upon our wilderness:
But we believe Thy faithful word,
And trust in our redeeming Lord.

99

101. O Jesus, I have promised.

1. O Jesus, I have prom-ised To serve Thee to the end;

Be Thou for ev-er near me, My Mas-ter and my Friend;

I shall not fear the bat-tle, If Thou art by my side,

Nor wan-der from the path-way, If Thou wilt be my Guide.

2 O Jesus, Thou hast promised
  To all who follow Thee,
That where Thou art in glory
  There shall Thy servant be ;
And, Jesus, I have promised
  To serve Thee to the end;
Oh give me grace to follow,
  My Master and my Friend.

3 Oh, let me see Thy foot-marks,
  And in them plant mine own;
My hope to follow duly
  Is in Thy strength alone ;
Oh guide me, call me, draw me,
  Uphold me to the end;
And then in heaven receive me,
  My Saviour and my Friend.

102   Jesus, I my Cross have taken.

1. Je - sus, I my cross have tak - en, All to leave, and fol - low Thee;
2. Let the world des - pise and leave me, They have left my Sav - iour too;

Des - ti - tute, des - pised, for - sak - en, Thou, from hence, my all shalt be.
Hu - man hearts and looks de - ceive me; Thou art not, like them, un - true.

Per - ish ev - er - y fond am - bi - tion, All I've sought, or hoped, or known;
And whilst Thou shalt smile up - on me, God of wis - dom, love and might!

Yet how rich is my con - di - tion! God and heaven are still my own.
Foes may hate and friends dis - own me; Show Thy face, and all is bright.

Saviour, blessed Saviour.

1. Sav - iour, bless - ed Sav - iour, Lis - ten while we sing, Hearts and voic-es
rais - ing Prais-es to our King. All we have to of - fer; All we hope to
be, Bo - dy, soul and spir - it, All we yield to Thee.

2 Nearer, ever nearer,
  Christ, we draw to Thee,
Deep in adoration,
  Bending low the knee.
Thou, for our redemption,
  Cam'st on earth to die;
Thou, that we might follow,
  Hast gone up on high.

3 Great, and ever greater,
  Are Thy mercies here;
True and everlasting
  Are the glories there;
Where no pain nor sorrow,
  Toil, nor care is known;
Where the angel-legions
  Circle round Thy throne.

104   My Faith looks up to Thee.

1. My faith looks up to Thee, Thou Lamb of Cal - va - ry: Sa -

- viour Di - vine: Now hear me while I pray; Take all my sins a -

- way; Oh let me from this day Be whol - ly Thine.

2 May Thy rich grace impart
  Strength to my fainting heart,
    My zeal inspire :
  As Thou hast died for me,
  Oh may my love to Thee
  Pure, warm and changeless be,
    A living fire.

3 When ends life's transient dream,
  When death's cold sullen stream
    Shall o'er me roll ;
  Blest Saviour, then in love,
  Fear and distrust remove ;
  Oh bear me safe above—
    A ransomed soul.

105   Rock of Ages, cleft for me.

1. { Rock of a - ges cleft for me. Let me hide my -
{ Let the wa - ter and the blood, From Thy riv - en

self in Thee: }
side which flowed, } Be of sin the dou - ble cure; Cleanse me

from its guilt and power, Cleanse me from its guilt and power.

Rock of ages, cleft for me.—Concluded.

2 Could my zeal no respite know,
  Could my tears forever flow,
  All for sin could not atone,
  Thou must save, and Thou alone;
  Nothing in my hand I bring;
  Simply to Thy cross I cling.

3 While I draw this fleeting breath,
  When my eyelids close in death,
  When I soar to worlds unknown,
  See Thee on Thy judgment throne;
  Rock of ages, cleft for me,
  Let me hide myself in Thee.

106   Lord, I confess to Thee.

1. Lord, I con-fess to Thee Sad-ly my sin; All I am tell I Thee, All I have been, Purge Thou my sin a-way,

slower.

Wash Thou my soul this day, Lord, make me clean.

2 Faithful and just art Thou,
  Forgiving all;
  Loving and kind art Thou,
  When poor ones call;
  Lord, let the cleansing blood,
  Blood of the Lamb of God
  Pass o'er my soul.

3 Then all is peace and light
  This soul within;
  Thus shall I walk with Thee,
  The loved unseen:
  Leaning on Thee, my God,
  Guided along the road,
  Nothing between.

107   O Jesus, Thou art standing.

1. O Je - sus, Thou art stand - ing Out - side the fast - closed door,

In low - ly pa - tience wait - ing To pass the thresh-old o'er;

Shame on us, Chris-tian breth - ren, His Name and sign who bear;

Oh shame, thrice shame up - on us, To keep Him stand - ing there.

2 O Jesus, Thou art knocking;
  And lo! that hand is scarr'd,
And thorns Thy brow encircle.
  And tears Thy face have marr'd:
O love that passeth knowledge,
  So patiently to wait!
O sin that hath no equal.
  So fast to bar the gate.

3 O Jesus, Thou art pleading
  In accents meek and low,
"I died for you, My children.
  And will you treat Me so?"
O Lord, with shame and sorrow
  We open now the door:
Dear Saviour, enter, enter.
  And leave us nevermore.

108 Jesus, Lover of my Soul.

1. Je - sus, lov - er of my soul, Let me to Thy bos - om fly,
2. Oth - er re - fuge have I none, Hangs my help-less soul on Thee;

While the near-er wa - ters roll, While the tem-pest still is high!
Leave, ah! leave me not a - lone, Still sup-port and com - fort me!

Hide me, O my Sav - iour, hide, Till the storm of life is past;
All my trust on Thee is stayed, All my help from Thee I bring;

Safe in - to the hav - en guide: Oh re - ceive my soul at last!
Cov - er my defence-less head With the sha - dow of Thy wing.

109   Jesus, the very Thought of Thee.

1. Je - sus, the ver - y thought of Thee With sweetness fills my breast;

But sweet - er far Thy face to see, And in Thy pres - ence rest.

2 O hope of every contrite heart!
   O joy of all the meek!
To those who fall, how kind Thou art!
   How good to those who seek!

3 Jesus, our only joy be Thou
   As Thou our crown wilt be;
Jesus, be Thou our glory now,
   And through eternity.

110   Take my Life, and let it be.

1. Take my life, and let it be Con - se - cra - ted, Lord, to Thee.
2. Take my hands, and let them move At the im - pulse of Thy love.

Take my Life, and let it be.—Concluded.

Take my mo - ments and my days, Let them flow in cease-less praise.
Take my feet and let them be Swift and beau - ti - ful for Thee.

3 Take my voice, and let me sing
Always, only, for my King.
Take my lips, and let them be
Filled with messages from Thee.

4 Take my love, my Lord, I pour
At Thy feet its treasured store.
Take myself, and I will be
Ever, only, all for Thee.

111 Jesus! I live to Thee.

1. Je - sus! I live to Thee, The love - li - est and best;
2. Je - sus! I die to Thee, When - ev - er death shall come;

My life in Thee, Thy life in me, In Thy blest love I rest.
To die in Thee is life to me In my e - ter - nal home.

3 Whether to live or die,
I know not which is best;
To live in Thee is bliss to me,
To die is endless rest.

4 Living or dying, Lord,
I ask but to be Thine:
My life in Thee, Thy life in me,
Makes heaven for ever mine.

1. Spir - it of God! descend up - on my heart; Wean it from earth; thro' all its puls - es move; Stoop to my weak - ness, migh-ty as Thou art, And make me love Thee as I ought to love.

2 Hast Thou not bid us love Thee, God and King?
   All, all Thine own — soul, heart and strength and mind;
  I see Thy cross — there teach my heart to cling!
  Oh let me see Thee, and Oh let me find!

3 Teach me to love Thee as Thine angels love,
  One holy passion filling all my frame :
  The kindling of the heaven-descending Dove,
  My heart an altar, and Thy love the flame.

O Love that casts out Fear.

1. O love that casts out fear, O love that casts out sin,
2. Great love of God, come in, Well-spring of heaven-ly peace;

Tar - ry no more with - out, But come and dwell with - in.
Thou Liv - ing Wa - ter, come, Spring up and nev - er cease.

True sun - light of the soul, Sur-round me as I go;
Love of the liv - ing God, Of Fa - ther and of Son,

So shall my way be safe, My feet no stray - ing know.
Love of the Ho - ly Ghost, Fill Thou each need - y one.

114　　They who on the Lord rely.

1. They who on the Lord re - ly, Safe - ly dwell, though dan-ger's nigh;

Lo! His shelt-'ring wings are spread, O'er each faith-ful ser-vant's head.

2 Vain temptation's wily snare;
Christian's are Jehovah's care;
Harmless flies the shaft by day,
Or in darkness wings its way.

3 When they wake, or when they sleep,
Angel guards their vigils keep;
Death and danger may be near;
Faith and love have nought to fear.

115　　Walk in the Light! so shalt thou know.

1. Walk in the light! so shalt thou know That fel - low - ship of love

Walk in the Light! so shalt thou know.—Concluded.

His spir-it on-ly can be-stow, Who reigns in light a-bove.

2 Walk in the light! and thou shalt find
   Thy heart made truly His,
Who dwells in cloudless light enshrined,
   In whom no darkness is.

3 Walk in the light! and thou shalt own
   Thy darkness passed away,
Because that Light hath on thee shone,
   In which is perfect day.

Copyright, 1886, by Cong'l S. S. and Pub. Soc.

116   Trustingly, trustingly.

1. Trustingly, trustingly, Je-sus, to Thee   Come I: Lord, lovingly Come Thou to me!
2. Peacefully, peacefully, Walk I with Thee;   Jesus, my Lord, Thou art All, all to me.

Then shall I lov-ing-ly, Then shall I joy-ful-ly, Walk here with Thee.
Peace Thou hast left us, Thy peace hast giv-en us; So let it be.

3 Whom but Thyself, O Lord!
   Have I above?
What have I left on earth?
   Only Thy love!
Come then, O Saviour! come:
Come then, O Spirit! come
   Heavenly Dove.

4 Happily, happily,
   Pass I along,
Eager to work for Thee,
   Earnest and strong.
Life is for service true,
Life is for battle too;
   Life is for song.

117   Just as I am.

1. Just as I am, with-out one plea, But that Thy blood was shed for me,
2. Just as I am, tho' tossed a - bout, With many a con - flict, many a doubt,

And that Thou bidd'st me come to Thee   O Lamb of God, I come, I come.
Fightings and fears, with-in, with-out,   O Lamb of God, I come, I come.

3 Just as I am,—Thou wilt receive,
Wilt welcome, pardon, cleanse, relieve;
Because Thy promise I believe,
O Lamb of God, I come.

4 Just as I am,—Thy love unknown
Has broken every barrier down;
Now to be Thine, yea, Thine alone,
O Lamb of God, I come.

118   While my Redeemer's near.

1 While my Re - deem - er's near, My Shep - herd and my Guide,
2. To ev - er fra - grant meads, Where rich a - bun - dance grows,

While my Redeemer's near.—Concluded.

I bid fare-well to anx-ious fear; My wants are all sup-plied.
His gra-cious hand in-dul-gent leads, And guards my sweet re-pose.

3 Dear Shepherd, if I stray,
   My wandering feet restore ;
To Thy fair pastures guide my way,
And let me rove no more.

4 Unworthy, as I am,
   Of Thy protecting care,
Jesus, I plead Thy gracious name,
For all my hopes are there.

119   Much in Sorrow, oft in Woe.

1. Much in sor-row, oft in woe, On-ward, Christians, on-ward go!
2. On-ward, Christians, on-ward go! Join the war, and face the foe;

Fight the fight, main-tain the strife, Strengthened with the bread of life.
Will ye flee in dan-ger's hour? Know ye not your Captain's pow'r?

3 Let your drooping hearts be glad ;
March, in heavenly armor clad ;
Fight, nor think the battle long,
Victory soon shall tune your song.

4 Onward, then, to battle move !
More than conquerors you shall prove :
Though opposed by many a foe,
Christian soldiers, onward go.

120   Work, for the Night is coming.

1. Work, for the night is com - ing; Work, thro' the morn-ing hours;

Work while the dew is spark - ling; Work 'mid spring-ing flowers:

Work, when the day grows bright - er; Work in the glow-ing sun;

Work, for the night is com - ing, When man's work is done.

2 Work, for the night is coming,
  Work through the sunny noon;
Fill brightest hours with labor,
  Rest comes sure and soon.
Give every flying minute
  Something to keep in store:
Work, for the night is coming,
  When man works no more.

3 Work, for the night is coming,
  Under the sunset skies;
While their bright tints are glowing,
  Work, for daylight flies.
Work till the last beam fadeth,
  Fadeth to shine no more:
Work while the night is darkening,
  When man's work is o'er.

Stand up! stand up for Jesus!

1. Stand up! stand up for Je - sus! Ye sol - diers of the cross;

Lift high His roy - al ban - ner, It must not suf - fer loss:

From vic - tory un - to vic - tory, His ar - my He shall lead,

Till ev - ery foe is van - quished, And Christ is Lord in - deed.

2 Stand up! stand up for Jesus!
  Stand in His strength alone;
The arm of flesh will fail you;
  Ye dare not trust your own:
Put on the gospel armor,
  And, watching unto prayer,
Where duty calls, or danger,
  Be never wanting there.

3 Stand up! stand up for Jesus!
  The strife will not be long;
This day the noise of battle,
  The next the victor's song:
To him that overcometh,
  A crown of life shall be;
He with the King of Glory
  Shall reign eternally.

Children of the Heavenly King.

SOLO.

1. Chil-dren of the Heavenly King, As ye jour-ney sweetly sing; Sing your Saviour's wor - thy praise, Glorious in His works and ways.

CHORUS.

1. We are travel-ling home to God, In the way the fa - thers trod:

Org. ped.

Children of the Heavenly King.—Concluded.

They are hap-py now, and we Soon their hap-pi-ness shall see.

2 Shout, ye little flock and blest;
You on Jesus' throne shall rest;
There your seat is now prepared:
There your kingdom and reward.
CHO.—Lord obediently we go,
Gladly leaving all below,
Only Thou our leader be.
And we still will follow Thee.

3 Lift your eyes, ye sons of light!
Zion's city is in sight:
There our endless home shall be,
There our Lord we soon shall see.
CHO.—Seal our love, our labors end;
Let us to Thy bliss ascend:
Let us to Thy kingdom come;
Lord! we long to be at home.

123   Blessed Saviour, Thee I love.

FINE.

1. Bles-sed Sav-iour, Thee I love, All my oth-er joys a-bove;
Ev-er let my glo-ry be, On-ly, on-ly, on-ly Thee.

D.C.

All my hopes in Thee a-bide, Thou my hope, and naught be-side;

2 Once again beside the cross,
All my gain I count but loss:—
Earthly pleasures fade away,—
Clouds they are that cloud my day.
Hence, vain shadows! let me see
Jesus, crucified for me.

3 Blessed Saviour, Thine am I,
Thine to live, and Thine to die;
Height or depth or earthly power,
Ne'er shall hide my Saviour more:
Ever shall my glory be,
Only, only, only Thee.

124   The Lord my Shepherd is.

1. The Lord my Shep - herd is,   I shall be   well sup - plied :
2. He leads me to   the place Where heaven-ly   pas - ture   grows,

Since He is mine and I   am His,   What can I   want be - side?
Where liv - ing wa - ters gen - tly   pass,   And full sal - va - tion flows.

3 If e'er I go astray,
    He doth my soul reclaim ;
    And guides me in His own right way,
    For His most holy name.

4 While He affords His aid,
    I cannot yield to fear :
    Though I should walk through death's dark
    My Shepherd's with me there. [shade,

125   As pants the Hart for cooling Streams.

1. As pants the hart for   cool - ing streams, When heat-ed in   the chase ;
2. For Thee, my God, the   liv - ing God, My thirs - ty soul doth pine ;

As pants the Hart for cooling Streams.—Concluded.

So longs my soul, O God, for Thee, And Thy re-fresh-ing grace.
Oh when shall I be-hold Thy face, Thou Ma-jes-ty di-vine?

3 I sigh to think of happier days,
   When Thou, O Lord, wert nigh;
   When every heart was tuned to praise,
   And none more blest than I.

4 Oh why art thou cast down my soul?
   Hope still, and thou shalt sing
   The praise of Him who is thy God,
   Thy health's eternal spring.

126   There is a Land of pure Delight.

1. There is a land of pure de-light, Where saints im-mor-tal reign,
2. There ev-er-last-ing spring a-bides, And nev-er-withering flowers;

In-fi-nite day ex-cludes the night, And pleas-ures ban-ish pain.
Death, like a nar-row sea, di-vides This heaven-ly land from ours.

3 Sweet fields beyond the swelling flood
   Stand dressed in living green;
   So to the Jews old Canaan stood,
   While Jordan rolled between.

4 Could we but climb where Moses stood,
   And view the landscape o'er,—
   Not Jordan's stream, nor death's cold flood,
   Should fright us from the shore.

    121

127   My Shepherd will supply my Need.

1. My Shep-herd will sup-ply my need; Je - ho - vah is His name:

In pas·tures fresh He makes me feed, Be-side the liv-ing stream.

2 He brings my wandering spirit back,
   When I forsake His ways:
   And leads me, for His mercy's sake.
   In paths of truth and grace.

3 When I walk through the shades of death,
   Thy presence is my stay:
   A word of Thy supporting breath
   Drives all my fears away.

4 The sure provisions of my God
   Attend me all my days;
   Oh may Thy house be mine abode.
   And all my work be praise.

5 There would I find a settled rest,
   While others go and come;
   No more a stranger or a guest,
   But like a child at home.

Sweet Alleluias !

1. Sweet Al - le - lu - ias ! the birds and the blos -soms Chant forth in har - mo-ny, "Praise to the Lord." Sweet Al - le - lu - ias from pen - i - tent bo - soms; And an - gels in rap - ture re - ech - o the word.

2 Sweet Alleluias ! the works of creation
    Praise Him Who only may e'er be adored ;
   Sweeter the thrill of a new animation
    When sinners, new pardoned, sing, " Praise to the Lord ! "

3 Sweet Alleluias to Jesus their Saviour:—
    All the bright seraphim join in the song :
   Nations shall start from their evil behavior,
    And sweet Alleluias to Jesus prolong.

4 Sweet Alleluias ! the great congregation
    Round the white throne shall re-echo the word,
   Pass with their palms through the gates of salvation,
    With sweet Alleluias in praise to the Lord.

129   Holy Bible, Book divine.

1. Ho - ly   Bi - ble, book di - vine, Pre - cious treas-ure, thou art mine!

Mine, to   tell   me   whence I   came! Mine, to teach me what I   am;

2 Mine, to chide me when I rove;
Mine, to show a Saviour's love;
Mine art thou to guide my feet;
Mine to judge, condemn, acquit.

3 Mine, to tell of joys to come,
And the rebel sinner's doom;
Holy Bible, book divine,
Precious treasure, thou art mine.

130   How precious is the Book divine.

1. How pre-cious is   the   book di - vine, By in - spi - ra - tion given!
2. It sweet-ly cheers our droop-ing hearts, In this dark vale of tears;

How precious is the Book divine.—Concluded.

Bright as a lamp its doc - trines shine, To guide our souls to heaven.
Life, light and joy it still im - parts, And quells our ris - ing fears.

3 O'er all the straight and narrow way
Its radiant beams are cast:
A light whose ever-cheering ray
Grows brightest at the last.

4 This lamp through all the tedious night
Of life shall guide our way;
Till we behold the clearer light
Of an eternal day.

131 Oh, could our Thoughts and Wishes fly.

1. Oh, could our thoughts and wish - es fly, A-bove these gloom-y shades,

To those bright worlds, be - yond the sky, Which sor - row ne'er in - vades.

2 Lord, send a beam of light divine,
To guide our upward aim:
With one reviving touch of Thine,
Our languid hearts inflame.

3 Then shall, on faith's sublimest wing,
Our ardent wishes rise
To those bright scenes, where pleasures
Immortal, in the skies.   [spring,

132   I love to tell the Story.

1. I love to tell the sto - ry Of un - seen things a - bove,
2. I love to tell the sto - ry; More won - der - ful it seems

Of Je - sus and His glo - ry, Of Je - sus and His love.
Than all the gold - en fan - cies Of all our gold - en dreams.

I love to tell the sto - ry, Be - cause I know it's true;
I love to tell the sto - ry; It did so much for me;

It sat - is - fies my long - ings As noth - ing else could do.
And that is just the rea - son I tell it now to thee.

I love to tell the Story.—Concluded.

CHORUS.

1. 2. 3. 4. I love to tell the sto - ry, 'Twill be my theme in glo - ry,

To tell the old, old sto - ry Of Je - sus and His love.

3. I love to tell the story;
   'Tis pleasant to repeat
What seems, each time I tell it,
   More wonderfully sweet.
I love to tell the story,
   For some have never heard
The message of salvation
   From God's own holy word.
I love to tell the story, etc.

4 I love to tell the story,
   For those who know it best
Seem hungering and thirsting
   To hear it, like the rest.
And when, in scenes of glory,
   I sing the new, new song,
'Twill be the old, old story,
   That I have loved so long.
I love to tell the story, etc.

133   I love to hear the Story.

1. I love to hear the sto - ry Which an - gel voi - ces tell,

I love to hear the Story.—Concluded.

How once the King of glo - ry Came down on earth to dwell.

I am both weak and sin - ful, But this I sure - ly know,

The Lord came down to save me Be-cause He loved me so.

2 I'm glad my blessed Saviour
  Was once a child like me,
To show how pure and holy
  His little ones might be;
And if I try to follow
  His footsteps here below,
He never will forget me,
  Because He loves me so.

3 To sing His love and mercy,
  My sweetest songs I'll raise;
And though I cannot see Him,
  I know He hears my praise;
For He has kindly promised
  That I shall surely go
To sing among His angels,
  Because He loves me so.

The Sands of Time are sinking.

1. The sands of time are sink - ing, The dawn of heav - en breaks.

The sum - mer morn I've sighed for, The fair, sweet morn a - wakes.

Dark, dark, hath been the mid - night, But day-spring is at hand,

And glo - ry, glo - ry, dwell - eth In Im - man - uel's land.

2 O Christ, He is the fountain,
  The deep, sweet well of love ;
The streams on earth I've tasted,
  More deep I'll drink above :
There, to an ocean fullness,
  His mercy doth expand,
And glory, glory dwelleth
  In Immanuel's land.

3 Oh, I am my Beloved's
  And my Beloved's mine ;
He brings a poor vile sinner,
  Into His house divine.
Upon the Rock of Ages
  My soul redeemed shall stand,
Where glory, glory dwelleth
  In Immanuel's land.

The Lord my Pasture shall prepare.

1. The Lord my pas - ture shall pre - pare, And feed me with a shepherd's care;

His pres - ence shall my wants sup - ply, And guard me with a watch - ful eye:

My noon-day walks He shall at - tend, And all my mid-night hours de-fend.

The Lord my Pasture shall prepare.—Concluded.

2 When in the sultry glebe I faint,
  Or on the thirsty mountain pant,
  To fertile vales and dewy meads
  My weary, wandering steps He leads,
  Where peaceful rivers, soft and slow,
  Amid the verdant landscape flow.

3 Though in the paths of death I tread,
  With gloomy horrors overspread,
  My steadfast heart shall fear no ill,
  For Thou, O Lord, art with me still:
  Thy friendly crook shall give me aid,
  And guide me through the dreadful shade.

136 What a strange and wondrous Story.

1. What a strange and wondrous sto - ry, From the book of God is read;
2. How He left His throne in heav-en, Here to suf - fer, bleed and die,

How the Lord of life and glo - ry Had not where to lay His head.
That my soul might be for - giv - en, And as - cend to God on high.

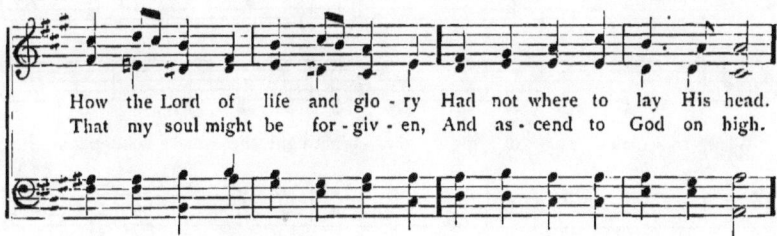

3 Father, let Thy Holy Spirit
  Still reveal a Saviour's love,
  And prepare me to inherit
  Glory where He reigns above.

4 There, with saints and angels dwelling,
  May I that great love proclaim,
  And with them be ever telling
  All the wonders of His name.

Jerusalem the Golden.

1. Je - ru - sa - lem the gold - en, With milk and hon - ey blest;

Be - neath thy con - tem - pla - tion Sink heart and voice op - pressed.

I know not, Oh, I know not, What joys a - wait me there;

What ra - dian - cy of glo - ry, What light be - yond com - pare.

2 They stand, those halls of Zion,
   All jubilant with song,
And bright with many an angel,
   And all the martyr throng:
The Prince is ever in them,
   The daylight is serene.
The pastures of the blessèd
   Are decked in glorious sheen.

3 There is the throne of David,
   And there, from care released,
The song of them that triumph,
   The shout of them that feast ;
And they, who with their Leader
   Have conquered in the fight,
For ever and for ever
   Are clad in robes of white.

138   There is a happy Land.

1. There is a hap-py land, Far, far a-way, Where saints in glo-ry stand,

Bright, bright as day. Oh, how they sweet-ly sing, Wor-thy is our

Sav-iour King, Loud let His prais-es ring, Praise, praise for aye!

2 Come to that happy land,
   Come, come away;
Why will ye doubting stand?
   Why still delay?
Oh, we shall happy be,
   When, from sin and sorrow free,
Lord, we shall live with Thee,
   Blest, blest for aye!

3 Bright, in that happy land,
   Beams every eye;
Kept by a Father's hand,
   Love cannot die.
Oh, then to glory run,
   Be a crown and kingdom won;
And bright above the sun,
   We reign for aye!

139 Above the clear blue Sky.

1. A - bove the clear blue sky, In heav - en's bright a - bode,
2. But God from in - fant tongues On earth re - ceiv - eth praise;

The an - gel host on high Sing prais - es to their God;
We then our cheer - ful songs In sweet ac - cord will raise:

Hal - le - lu - jah! They love to sing to God their King Hal-le-lu - jah!
Hal - le - lu - jah! We too will sing to God our King Hal-le-lu - jah!

134

Above the clear blue Sky.—Concluded.

3 O blessed Lord, Thy truth
  To us Thy babes impart,
And teach us in our youth
  To know Thee as Thou art.
    Hallelujah!
  Then shall we sing to God our King
    Hallelujah!

4 Oh may Thy holy word
  Spread all the earth around;
And all with one accord
  Uplift the joyful sound.
    Hallelujah!
  All then shall sing to God their King
    Hallelujah!

140 There is a River, deep and broad.

1. There is a riv-er, deep and broad, Its course no mor-tal knows;
2. Clear-er than crys-tal is the stream, And bright with end-less day;

It fills with joy the church of God, And wid-ens as it flows.
The waves with ev-ery bless-ing teem, And life and health con-vey.

3 Where'er they flow contentions cease,
  And love and meekness reign;
The Lord himself commands the peace,
  And foes conspire in vain.

4 Along the shores, angelic bands
  Watch every moving wave;
With holy joy their breast expands,
  When men the waters crave.

5 To them distressèd souls repair,
  The Lord invites them nigh:
They leave their cares and sorrows there,
  They drink, and never die.

6 Flow on, sweet stream, more largely flow,
  The earth with glory fill;
Flow on, till all the Saviour know,
  And all obey His will.

141   O Paradise.

1. O Par - a - dise! O Par - a - dise! Who doth not crave for rest?
2. O Par - a - dise! O Par - a - dise! The world is grow - ing old!

Who would not seek the hap - py land Where they that loved are bless'd,
Who would not be at rest and free Where love is nev - er cold?

Where loy - al hearts and true

Where loy - al hearts and true Stand ev - er in the light,

All rap-ture through and through, In God's most ho - ly sight. A - men.

3 O Paradise! O Paradise!
   Wherefore doth death delay?
Bright death, that is the welcome dawn
   Of our eternal day;
     Where loyal hearts, etc.

4 O Paradise! O Paradise!
   'Tis weary waiting here:
I long to be where Jesus is,
   To feel, to see Him near.
     Where loyal hearts, etc. Amen.

There is a Land immortal.

1. There is a land im-mor-tal, The beau-ti-ful of lands; Be-side its an-cient por-tal A si-lent sen-try stands; He on-ly can un-do it, And o-pen wide the door; And mortals who pass through it Are mor-tals nev-er-more.

2 Though dark and drear the passage
   That leadeth to the gate,
Yet grace attends the message
   To souls that watch and wait:
And at the time appointed,
   A messenger comes down,
And guides the Lord's anointed
   From cross to glory's crown.

3 Their sighs are lost in singing,
   They're blessèd in their tears;
Their journey heavenward winging,
   They leave on earth their fears:
Death like an angel seemeth;
   "We welcome thee," they cry;
Their face with glory beameth—
   'Tis life for them to die!

143   # For thee, O dear, dear Country.

1. For thee, O dear, dear coun-try, Mine eyes their vig-ils keep;

For ver-y love, be-hold-ing Thy hap-py name, they weep.

The men-tion of Thy glo-ry, Is unc-tion to the breast,

And med-i-cine in sick-ness, And love and life and rest.

2 The Lamb is all thy splendor,
  The Crucified thy praise;
His laud and benediction
  Thy ransomed people raise.
And He whom now we trust in,
  Shall then be seen and known;
And they that know and see Him
  Shall have Him for their own.

3 I know not — oh, I know not
  What social joys are there,
What radiancy of glory,
  What light beyond compare !
And when I fain would sing them,
  My spirit fails and faints,
And vainly tries to image
  The assembly of the saints.

Ten thousand times ten thousand.

1. Ten thous - and times ten thous - and, In spark - ling rai · ment bright,

The ar - mies of the ransomed saints Throng up the steeps of light:

'Tis fin - ished! all is fin - ished, Their fight with death and sin; ...

Fling o - pen wide the gold - en gates, And let the vic - tors in.

2 What rush of hallelujahs
   Fills all the earth and sky !
   What ringing of a thousand harps
   Bespeaks the triumph nigh !
   O day, for which creation
   And all its tribes were made !
   O joy, for all its former woes
   A thousand-fold repaid.

3 Oh, then what raptured greetings
   On Canaan's happy shore !
   What knitting severed friendships up,
   Where partings are no more !
   Then eyes with joy shall sparkle,
   That brimmed with tears of late :
   Orphans no longer fatherless,
   Nor widows desolate.

145   From Greenland's icy Mountains.

1. From Greenland's i-cy mountains, From India's cor-al strand; Where Afric's sun-ny

foun - tains Roll down their gold-en sand: From many an an-cient riv - er, From

many a palm-y plain; They call us to de - liv - er Their land from er -ror's

chain, They call us to de - liv - er Their land from er - ror's chain.

2 Can we, whose souls are lighted
   With wisdom from on high,
Can we to man benighted
   The lamp of life deny?
Salvation, Oh, salvation!
   The joyful sound proclaim,
Till earth's remotest nation
   Has learned Messiah's name.

3 Waft, waft, ye winds His story,
   And you, ye waters, roll,
Till, like a sea of glory,
   It spreads from pole to pole;
Till o'er our ransomed nature,
   The Lamb, for sinners slain,
Redeemer, King, Creator,
   In bliss return to reign.

146   Very swiftly bear Thine Angels.

1. Ver-y swift-ly bear Thine an-gels, God on High, Thy glad e - van - gels,

The first meaning of the word angel is messenger.

Shed - ding gold and a - zure light From their wings in rap - id flight:

Find - ing in Thy ser - vice blest Their supreme and per - fect rest;

May we do Thy bid - ding, e - ven As Thy will is done in Heav-en.

2 Very stainless are Thine angels,
Bearing on Thy glad evangels;
Though their errand calleth them
From the New Jerusalem
Into regions dark and wild,
Still their robes are undefiled:
May we do Thy bidding, even
As Thy will is done in Heaven.

3 Children, too, may be Thine angels,
Bearing on Thy glad evangels;
Beautiful may be our feet
On the mountains, for the sweet
Tidings of great joy we bring
From the palace of the King:
We may do Thy bidding, even
As Thy will is done in Heaven.

    141

1. Je - sus shall reign wher - e'er the sun Doth his suc - ces - sive jour - neys run; His king - dom stretch from shore to shore, Till moons shall wax and wane no more, Till moons shall wax and wane no more.

2 For Him shall endless prayer be made,
And praises throng to crown His head;
His name like sweet perfume shall rise
With every morning sacrifice.

3 People and realms of every tongue
Dwell on His love with sweetest song;
And infant voices shall proclaim
Their early blessings on His name.

4 Blessings abound where'er He reigns;
The prisoner leaps to lose his chains;
The weary find eternal rest,
And all the sons of want are blest.

5 Let every creature rise and bring
Peculiar honors to our King;
Angels descend with songs again,
And earth repeat the long Amen.

142

148 Oh, where are Kings and Empires now.

1. Oh, where are kings and em-pires now Of old that went and came?
2. We mark her good-ly bat-tle-ments And her found-a-tions strong;

But, Lord, Thy church is pray-ing yet, A thou-sand years the same.
We hear with-in the sol-emn voice Of her un-end-ing song.

3 For not like kingdoms of the world
  Thy holy church, O God!
  Though earthquake shocks are threatening her,
  And tempests are abroad;

4 Unshaken as eternal hills,
  Immovable she stands,
  A mountain that shall fill the earth,
  A house not made by hands.

149 **Come and sing.**

1. Come, and sing with joy and gladness, El - e - vate your hearts in praise,
2. Come, and sweet-ly tune your voi - ces, Raise them to a loft - y strain;

Come, dis-miss all gloom and sad-ness, High your songs ex - ult-ing raise:
Sing a - loud while Heaven re-joic - es, Shout! for Je - sus comes to reign;

With an - gel - ic choirs u - nit-ing, Sing of Je - sus' won-drous love;
Glo - ry, hear the an - gels cry-ing Glo - ry to the Sav-iour's name;

List! the an - gels' song in - vit-ing Will-ing souls to joys a - bove.
Shall not chil - dren with them vy - ing, Here on earth His praise pro-claim.

FESTIVALS AND SEASONS.

Peace on Earth.

Slow.

p

1. Peace on earth! The mor - row bring - eth mirth.

p Unison.

The night-tide bringeth us slumbers deep, By His dear grace Who shared our sleep

p

rall e dim.

Once on earth, Once on earth.

2 Here on earth
   Our Saviour suffered birth,
While angels smote their harps of flame,
And thrilled the stars with glad acclaim:
   Peace on earth.

3 May His peace
   Upon the earth increase,
Till all hearts bow to His diadem,
And hail the Babe of Bethlehem,
   Prince of Peace.

145

151 It came upon the Midnight clear.

1. It came up-on the mid-night clear,—That glo-rious song of old,

From an-gels bend-ing near the earth To touch their harps of gold:

"Peace on the earth; good-will to men From Heaven's all - gra-cious King!"

The world in sol-emn still-ness lay To hear the an-gels sing,

2 Still through the cloven skies they come
   With peaceful wings unfurled;
And still their heavenly music floats
   O'er all the weary world;
Above its sad and lowly plains
   They bend on hovering wing,
And ever o'er its Babel-sounds
   The blessed angels sing.

3 For lo! the days are hastening on,
   By prophet-bards foretold,
When with the ever-circling years.
   Comes round the age of gold;
When peace shall over all the earth
   Its ancient splendors fling,
And the whole world send back the song
   Which now the angels sing.

Angels from the realms of Glory.

1. An-gels from the realms of glo-ry, Wing your flight o'er all the earth;
2. Shep-herds in the field a-bid-ing, Watch-ing o'er your flocks by night,

Ye who sang cre-a-tion's sto-ry, Now pro-claim Mes-si-ah's birth;
God with man is now re-sid-ing, Yon-der shines the in-fant light;

Come and wor-ship; Wor-ship Christ, the new--born King.
Come and wor-ship; Wor-ship Christ, the new--born King.

3 Saints before the altar bending,
  Watching long in hope and fear,
Suddenly, the Lord descending,
  In His temple shall appear;
  Come and worship;
Worship Christ, the new-born King.

4 Sinners, wrung with true repentance,
  Doomed for guilt to woful pains,
Justice now revokes the sentence,
  Mercy calls you—break your chains:
  Come and worship;
Worship Christ, the new-born King.

153   Hark! the herald Angels sing.

1. Hark! the her - ald an - gels sing   Glo - ry   to   the   new born King; Peace on
2. Hail, the heav'n-born Prince of Peace! Hail, the Sun   of   Righteousness! Light and

earth and mer-cy   mild, God and sin -ners rec-on- ciled. Joy-ful, all ye na-tions
life   to all He brings, Risen with healing in His wings, Mild He lays His glo- ry

rise, Join the triumph of the skies; With the angelic host pro-claim Christ is
by,   Born that man no more may die. Born to raise the sons of earth, Born to

born   in Beth-lehem. Hark! the her -ald an-gels sing   Glo-ry   to   the new-born King.
give them second birth. Hark! the her - ald an-gels sing   Glo-ry   to   the new born King.

Org

148

Waken, Christian Children.

154

Solo.

1 Wak-en! Christ-ian chil - dren, Up and let us
2. Come, nor fear to seek Him, Chil-dren though we

Allegretto.

sing, With glad voice the prais - es,
be; Once He said of chil - dren,

Of our new-born King— Of our new-born King.
"Let them come to me," "Let them come to me."

149

Waken, Christian Children.—Continued.

1. Up! 'tis meet to wel - come With a joy - ous lay, ...
2. In a man - ger low - ly Sleeps the Heaven-ly child: . . .

Christ, the King of Glo - ry, Born for us to - day.
O'er Him fond - ly bend - eth, Ma - ry, Moth - er mild.

150

Waken, Christian Children.—Concluded.

2 Fear not then to enter.
  Though we cannot bring,
  Gold, or myrrh, or incense
  Fitting for a King—

CHO. Gifts he asketh richer,
  Offerings costlier still,
  Yet may Christian children
  Bring them if they will.

3 Brighter than all jewels
  Shines the modest eye,
  Best of gifts He loveth
  Infant purity—

CHO. Haste we then to welcome
  With a joyous lay
  Christ, the King of Glory,
  Born for us to-day.

155 While Shepherds watched their Flocks by Night.

1. While shepherds watched their flocks by night, All seat - ed on the ground,
2. "Fear not," said he, for migh - ty dread Had seized their trou - bled mind;

The an - gel of the Lord came down, And glo - ry shone a - round.
"Glad tid - ings of great joy I bring To you and all man - kind.

3 " To you in David's town this day
  Is born, of David's line,
  A Saviour, who is Christ the Lord;
  And this shall be the sign :"

4 " The heavenly Babe you there shall find
  To human view displayed,
  All meanly wrapped in swathing bands,
  And in a manger laid."

5 Thus spake the seraph ; and forthwith
  Appeared a shining throng
  Of angels, praising God, and thus
  Addressed their joyful song :

6 " All glory be to God on high,
  And to the earth be peace ;
  Good will henceforth from heaven to men
  Begin, and never cease."

Moderato.

mf

1. All this night bright an - gels sing, Nev - er was such ca - rol - ing,
2. Wake, O earth, wake ev - ery-thing, Wake, and hear the joy I bring:

cres.   *f*

Hark! a voice which loud - ly cries, "Mor - tals, mor - tals, wake and
Wake and joy; for all this night, Heaven and ev - ery twink - ling

p   *cres.*

rise. Lo! to glad - ness Turns your sad - ness; From the earth is
light, All a - maz - ing, Still stand gaz - ing; An - gels, Pow'rs and

f

risen a sun, Shines all night, though day .... be done.
all that be, Wake, and joy this Sun .... to see!

All this Night bright Angels sing.—Concluded.

3. Hail! O Sun, O bless - ed Light, Sent in - to this world by night;

Let Thy rays and heav - enly powers, Shine in these dark souls of

ours. For most du - ly, Thou art tru - ly God and man, we

do con - fess; Hail, O Sun of Right - eous - ness!

157   Child Jesus.

1. Child Je-sus came from Heav'n to earth, The Father's mer-cy
2. O soul with sin and grief cast down, For-get thy bit-ter

show - ing; In sta - ble mean He had His birth, No bet - ter cra - dle
sad - ness! A Child is come to Da - vid's town, To bring thee joy and

know - ing; A star smiled down the Babe to greet; The hum - ble ox - en
glad - ness! Oh, let us haste the Child to find, And child - like be in

Child Jesus.—Concluded.

kissed His feet, All praise to Thee, All praise to Thee, Child Je - sus!
heart and mind, All praise to Thee, All praise to Thee, Child Je - sus!

158   From Heaven above to Earth I come.

1. From heaven a - bove to earth I come, To bear good news to ev -'ry home;
2. To you this night is born a Child Of Ma - ry, cho - sen Moth-er mild;

Glad tid - ings of great joy I bring. Where-of I now will say and sing:
This lit - tle Child of low - ly birth Shall be the joy of all your earth.

3 Were earth a thousand times as fair,
Beset with gold and jewels rare,
She yet were far too poor to be
A narrow cradle, Lord, for Thee.

Written by Martin Luther for his son Hans.

4 Ah, dearest Jesus, holy Child,
Make Thee a bed, soft, undefiled
Within my heart, that it may be
A quiet chamber kept for Thee.

Oh come, all ye faithful.

1. Oh come. all ye faith - ful, Joy-ful - ly tri - um - phant, To Beth - le - hem has - ten now with glad ac - cord; Lo! in a man - ger Sits the King of an - gels; Oh come, let us a-dore Him, Oh come let us a-dore Him, Oh come, let us a - dore Him, Christ the Lord.

2 Raise, raise, choirs of angels!
Songs of loudest triumph,
Through heaven's high arches be your praises
Now to our God be   [poured;
Glory in the highest;
Oh come, etc.

3 Amen! Lord we bless Thee,
Born for our salvation,
O Jesus! forever be Thy name adored,
Word of the Father.
Late in flesh appearing:
Oh come, etc.

160   In the Country nigh to Bethlehem.

Allegretto.

1. In the coun - try nigh to Beth - lehem, On a star - ry night of
2. As they watched, a burst of glo - ry Shone a - round them from a -

old, There were in the fields a - bid - ing Shep - herds with their flocks in
bove, And a migh - ty glo-rious An - gel Calmed their fears with words of

fold. Round the flocks the faith - ful shep-herds Kept their watch from eve till
love: "Fear not, for be - hold I bring you Ti - dings full of great - est

morn, Lest their sheep so weak and help-less, Should by e - vil beasts be torn.
joy, Joy e - ter - nal, full of glad-ness, Joy which noth - ing can de-stroy.

In the Country nigh to Bethlehem.—Concluded.

3 "Unto you in David's city,
  As was told by Prophet's word,
Christ is born, your God and Saviour,
  Christ is born, your King and Lord."
Suddenly a host of Angels
  Raised their voices high and sang,
Till the vaulted arch of Heaven
  With the echoing chorus rang:

4 "Glory, glory in the highest,
  Unto God, and peace on earth;
To all nations joyful bring we
  Tidings glad of Jesus' birth."
Lift we now our hearts and voices,
  Join we all the cheerful cry,
Learned by shepherds from the Angels:
  "Glory be to God on high."

161   Ring the Bells, the Christmas Bells.

1. Ring the bells, the Christmas bells; Chime out the wondrous sto - ry;

First in song on an - gel tongues It came from realms of glo - ry;

Peace on earth, good will to men, An - gel - ic voi - ces ring - ing—

Ring the Bells, the Christmas Bells.—Concluded.

rall.

Christ the Lord to earth has come, His glo - rious mes - sage bring - ing.

f CHORUS.

Ring the mer - ry Christmas bells; Chime out the won drous sto - ry;

ff

Glo - ry be to God on high, For ev - er - more be glo - ry,

2 Wise men hastened from the East
   To bring their richest treasures—
Gold and myrrh and frankincense,
   And jewels without measure.
Him they sought, although a King,
   They found in birth-place lowly,
There within a manger lay
   The Babe so pure and holy.

3 Earthly crowns were not for Him;
   He came God's love revealing;
On the cross He died for us,
   His blood forgiveness sealing.
'Tis the Saviour promised long,
   Ring out your loudest praises;
Every heart this happy day
   Its grateful anthem raises.

162 Brightest and best of the Sons of the Morning.

1. Bright - est and best of the sons of the morn - ing, Dawn on our
2. Cold on His cra - dle the dew - drops are shin - ing; · Low lies His

dark - ness, and lend us thine aid! Star of the East, the ho -
head with the beasts of the stall; An - gels a - dore Him, in

ri - zon a - dorn - ing, Guide where our in - fant Re-deem - er is laid.
slum - ber re - clin - ing, Ma - ker, and Mon - arch, and Sav - iour of all.

3 Say, shall we yield Him, in costly devotion,
  Odors of Edom and offerings divine,
  Gems of the mountain, and pearls of the ocean,
  Myrrh from the forest, or gold from the mine?

4 Vainly we offer each ample oblation;
  Vainly with gifts would His favor secure;
  Richer by far is the heart's adoration;
  Dearer to God are the prayers of the poor.

Once in royal David's City.

1. Once in roy - al Dav - id's Ci - ty Stood a low - ly cat - tle shed,
2. And thro' all His won-drous childhood, He would hon - or and o - bey,

Where a moth - er laid her Ba - by, In a man - ger for His bed;
Love and watch the low - ly mai - den In whose gen - tle arms He lay;

Ma - ry was that moth - er mild Je - sus Christ her lit - tle Child.
Christ - ian child - ren all must be Mild, o - be - dient, good as He.

3 For He is our childhood's pattern,
　Day by day like us He grew;
　He was little, weak and helpless,
　Tears and smiles like us He knew;
　And He feeleth for our sadness,
　And He shareth in our gladness.

4 And our eyes at last shall see Him,
　Through His own redeeming love,
　For that Child so dear and gentle
　Is our Lord in heaven above;
　And He leads His children on
　To the place where He is gone.

When Christ was born of Mary free.

SOLO.

1. When Christ was born of Ma - ry free, In
2. Herdsmen beheld these an - gels bright, To

Beth - le - hem that fair ci - tie, An - gels sang there with
them ap - pear - ing with great light, Who said God's Son is

mirth and glee, An - gels sang there with mirth and glee,
born to - night, Who said God's Son is born to - night,

When Christ was born of Mary free.—Concluded.

"In ex-cel-sis Glo-ri-a," In ex-cel-sis Glo-ri-a,

In ex-cel-sis Glo-ri-a, In ex-cel-sis Glo-ri-a.

3 The King is come to save mankind,
   As in the Scripture truths we find,
   Therefore this song we have in mind—
   "In excelsis Gloria."

4 Then, dear Lord, for Thy great grace,
   Grant us in bliss to see Thy face
   That we may sing to Thy solace,
   "In excelsis Gloria."

163

165   Dropping, dropping, dropping.

1. Drop - ping, drop - ping, drop-ping, Slow - ly dropping a - way;
2. Drop - ping, drop - ping, drop-ping, No sound of spok - en word;

Like the si - lent sands of the hour-glass, Drops the old year day by day.
But ev - 'ry day had a tale to tell, Which on - ly God has heard.

3 Dropping, dropping, dropping,
   Swiftly dropping away:
   So go the years of the early life
   On their appointed way.

4 Dropping, dropping, dropping,
   Oh, joy to see them go,
   If they tell a tale in our Father's ear
   Of a holy light below.

166   While with ceaseless Course the Sun.

1. While with cease - less course the sun, Hast - ed through the for - mer year,

While with ceaseless Course the Sun.—Concluded.

Man - y souls their race have run, Nev-er more to meet us here,

Fixed in an e - ter - nal state, They have done with all be - low;

We a lit - tle long - er wait; But how lit - tle none can know.

2 As the wingèd arrow flies,
  Speedily the mark to find,
As the lightning from the skies
  Darts, and leaves no trace behind ;
Swiftly thus our fleeting days
  Bear us down life's rapid stream ;
Upward, Lord, our spirits raise ;
  All below is but a dream.

3 Thanks for mercies past receive ;
  Pardon of our sins renew ;
Teach us henceforth how to live
  With eternity in view.
Bless Thy word to young and old :
  Fill us with a Saviour's love ;
And when life's short tale is told,
  May we dwell with Thee above.

Standing at the Portal.

1. Stand - ing at the por - tal Of the o - pening year,
2. I the Lord am with thee, Be not thou a - fraid!

Words of com - fort meet us, Hush - ing ev - ery fear;
I will help and strength - en, Be not thou dis - mayed!

Spok - en through the si - lence, By our Fa - ther's voice,
Yea, I will up - hold thee With My own Right Hand:

Ten - der, strong and faith - ful Mak - ing us re - joice.
Thou art called and chos - en, In My sight to stand.

Standing at the Portal.—Concluded.

CHORUS. 1. 2. 3. 4.

On - ward then, and fear not, Chil - dren of the Day!

ritard.

For His word shall nev - er, Nev - er pass a - way.

3 For the year before us,
  Oh, what rich supplies!
For the poor and needy,
  Living streams shall rise;
For the sad and sinful
  Shall His grace abound;
For the faint and feeble
  Perfect strength be found.—CHO.

4 He will never fail us,
  He will not forsake;
His eternal covenant
  He will never break.
Resting on His promise,
  What have we to fear?
God is all sufficient
  For the coming year.—CHO.

168   Great God, we sing that mighty Hand.

1. Great God, we sing that might-y hand By which sup-port-ed still we stand:

Great God, we sing that mighty Hand.—Concluded.

The open-ing year Thy ·mer-cy shows, Let mer-cy crown it till it close.

2 By day, by night, at home, abroad,
  Still are we guarded by our God;
  By His incessant bounty fed,
  By His unerring counsel led.

3 With grateful hearts the past we own ;
  The future, all to us unknown,
  We to Thy guardian care commit,
  Content with what Thou deemest fit.

169 The Winter is over and gone.

1. The win-ter is o-ver and gone, The thrush whistles sweet on the spray,
2. Shall ev-er-y creature a-round Their voi-ces in con-cert u-nite,

The tur-tle breathes forth her soft moan, The lark mounts and warbles a-way.
And I, the most fa-vored, be found In prais-ing to take less de-light?

3 Awake, then, my harp and my lute :
  Sweet organs, your notes softly swell;
  No longer my lips shall be mute,
  The Saviour's high praises to tell.

4 His love in my heart shed abroad,
  My graces shall bloom as the spring;
  This temple, His spirit's abode
  My joy, as my duty, to sing.

170 When Verdure clothes the fertile Vale.

1. When ver - dure clothes the fer - tile vale, And blos - soms deck the spray; .... And fra - grance breathes in ev - ery gale, How sweet the ver - nal day! ...

2 Hark! how the feathered warblers sing!
  'Tis nature's cheerful voice:
  Soft music hails the lovely spring,
  And woods and fields rejoice.

3 O God of nature and of grace,
  Thy heavenly gifts impart:
  Then shall my meditation trace
  Spring, blooming in my heart.

4 Inspired to praise, I then shall join
  Glad nature's cheerful song;
  And love and gratitude divine
  Attune my joyful tongue.

When, His Salvation bringing.

1. When, His sal - va - tion bring - ing, To Zi - on Je - sus came,

The chil-dren all stood sing - ing Ho - san - nas to His name.

Nor did their zeal of - fend Him, But, as He rode a - long,

He let them still at - tend Him, And smiled to hear their song.

When, His Salvation bringing.—Concluded.

Fling out, fling out the ban - ner Of Christ, our heav - enly King;

Ring out, ring out Ho - san - na, And Hal - le - lu - jah sing.

2 And since the Lord retaineth
  His love for children still,
Though now as King He reigneth
  On Zion's heavenly hill;
We'll flock around His banner.
  Who sits upon the throne,
And cry aloud Hosanna
  To David's royal Son.—Cho.

3 For should we fail proclaiming
  Our great Redeemer's praise,
The stones, our silence shaming,
  Would their hosannas raise.
But shall we only render
  The tribute of our words?
No! while our hearts are tender,
  They too shall be the Lord's.—Cho.

171

Hosanna we sing!

1. Ho - san - na we sing, like the chil - dren dear, In the old - en days when the Lord lived here; He blessed lit - tle children and smiled on them, When they chanted His praise in Je - ru - sa - lem.

Hal - le - lu - jah we sing, like the chil - dren bright, With their

Hosanna we sing!—Concluded.

harps of gold and their rai-ment white; As they fol-low their Shepherd with

lov - ing eyes Through the beau-ti-ful val-leys of Par - a - dise,

Through the beau - ti - ful val - leys of Par - a - dise.

2 Hosanna we sing, for He bends His ear,
  And rejoices the hymns of His own to hear:
  We know that His heart will never wax cold
  To the lambs that He feeds in His earthly fold.
  Hallelujah we sing in the Church we love,
  Hallelujah resounds in the Church above;
  To Thy little ones, Lord, may such grace be given,
  That we lose not our part in the song of Heaven.

173

173 O sacred Head, now wounded.

1. O sa - cred Head, now wound - ed, With grief and shame cast

down, ... So scorn - ful - ly sur - round - ed,

With thorns Thine on - ly crown; . . . How art Thou pale with

O sacred Head, now wounded.—Concluded.

an - guish, With sore a - buse and scorn! How do those

feat - ures lan - guish, Which once were fair as morn. . . .

2 What language shall I borrow
   To thank Thee, dearest Friend,
For this Thy dying sorrow,
   This love that knew no end?
Oh, make me Thine forever!
   And should I fainting be,
Lord, let me never, never
   Out-live my love to Thee.

174   There is a green Hill far away.

1. There is a green hill far a-way, With-out a cit-y wall,
Where the dear Lord was cru-ci-fied, Who died to save us all....
We may not know, we can-not tell, What pain He had to bear.
But we be-lieve it was for us He hung and suf-fered there.

2 He died that we might be forgiven,
   He died to make us good,
That we might go at last to heaven,
   Saved by His precious blood.
There was no other good enough
   To pay the price of sin;
He only could unlock the gate
   Of Heaven, and let us in.

3 Oh dearly, dearly has He loved,
   And we must love Him too,
And trust in His redeeming blood,
   And try His works to do.
For there's a green hill far away,
   Without a city wall,
Where the dear Lord was crucified,
   Who died to save us all.

Songs of Gladness, songs of Praise.

1. Songs of glad-ness, songs of praise, To God on high be giv - en,

Shouts of tri - umph let us raise, For Death's dark chains are riv - en;

Night and gloom hung dark and drear - y, O'er the world that sol - emn night,

Weep - ing friends with watch-ing wea - ry, Sought the tomb at morn - ing light.

2 As the sun through eastern skies,
　Breaks forth as from a prison,
So our doubts, our darkness flies,
　For Christ, our Lord, is risen;
Angels bright, with heavenly glory,
　Shining through that narrow room,
Stayed to tell the wondrous story,
　"Seek him not within the tomb."

3 While the birds with cheerful song
　Rejoice that spring is breaking,
After winter, cold and long,
　Our earth to life awaking;
Never more with doubt and sadness,
　But with praise and sweet accord,
With deep joy and heart-felt gladness,
　Let us seek our risen Lord.

　　177

Hail the Day that sees Him rise.

1. Hail the day that sees Him rise, Al - le - lu - ia! To His throne a -
2. There for Him high tri - umph waits, Al - le - lu - ia! Lift your heads, e -

- bove the skies; Al - le - lu - ia! Christ the Lamb, for sin - ners given,
- ter - nal gates; Al - le - lu - ia, O - pen wide: He en - ters in,

Al - le - lu - ia! En - ters now the high-est heaven. Al - le - lu - ia.
Al - le - lu - ia! Con - quer-or of death and sin. Al - le - lu - ia.

3 Lo, the heaven its Lord receives,
    Alleluia!
Yet He loves the earth He leaves;
    Alleluia!
Though returning to His throne,
    Alleluia!
Still He calls mankind His own.
    Alleluia!

4 Lord, though parted from our sight,
    Alleluia!
Far above the starry height,
    Alleluia!
Grant our hearts may thither rise,
    Alleluia!
Seeking Thee above the skies.
    Alleluia!

Hallelujah! Hallelujah!

1. Hal - le - lu - jah! Hal - le - lu - jah! Hearts to heaven and voi-ces raise;

Sing to God a hymn of glad-ness, Sing to God a hymn of praise:

He, Who on the cross a vic - tim For the world's sal - va - tion bled,

Je - sus Christ, the King of glo - ry, Now is ris - en from the dead.

2 Christ is risen, we are risen!
  Shed upon us heavenly grace,
Rain and dew and gleams of glory
  From the brightness of Thy face:
So that we, with hearts in heaven,
  Here on earth may fruitful be,
And by angel-hands be gathered,
  And be ever, Lord, with Thee.

3 Hallelujah! Hallelujah!
  Glory be to God on high;
Hallelujah to the Saviour,
  Who has gained the victory;
Hallelujah to the Spirit,
  Fount of love and sanctity;
Hallelujah! Hallelujah!
  To the Triune Majesty.

178   Awake, thou wintry Earth.

1. A - wake, thou win - try earth! Fling off thy sad -
2. Wave, woods, your blos - soms all! Grim death is

ness! Fair ver - nal flowers, laugh forth Your an - cient glad - ness:
dead: Ye weep-ing, fun - eral trees, Lift up, lift up your head.

CHORUS.

Christ is ris - en! Christ is ris - en! Christ is ris - en! Christ is ris'n, is ris - en!

3 All is fresh and new,
   Full of spring and light:
   Wintry heart, why wear'st the hue,
   The hue of sleep and night?—CHO.

4 Leave thy cares beneath,
   Leave thy worldly love:
   Begin the better life
   With God, with God above.—CHO.

    180

179   Come, ye Faithful, raise the Strain.

1. Come, ye faith-ful, raise the strain Of triumphant gladness; God hath brought His

Is - ra - el   In - to joy from sad - ness; Loosed from Pharaoh's bit - ter yoke

Jacob's sons and daughters; Led them with unmoistened feet Thro' the Red Sea wa-ters.

2 'Tis the spring of souls to-day:
   Christ hath burst His prison,
And from three days' sleep in death,
   As the sun, hath risen :
All the winter of our sins,
   Long and dark, is flying
From His light to whom we give
   Laud and praise undying.

3 Now the Queen of seasons, bright
   With the Day of splendor,
With the royal Feast of Feasts,
   Comes its joy to render;
Comes to glad Jerusalem,
   Which with true affection
Welcomes in unwearied strains
   Jesus' resurrection.

He is risen!

1. He is ris - en! He is ris - en! Tell it with a joy - ful voice;

He hath burst His three days' pris - on! Let the whole wide earth re - joice:

Death is conquered, man is free, Christ has won the vic - to - ry.

2 Come with high and holy gladness,
  Chant our Lord's triumphal lay;
Not one touch of twilight sadness
  Dims the glorious morning ray,
Breaking o'er the purple east,
Symbol of our joyous feast.

3 He is risen! He is risen!
  He hath opened heaven's gate;
We are free from sin's dark prison—
  Risen to a holier state;
Soon a brighter Easter beam
On our longing eyes shall stream.

181   Jesus lives! no longer now.

1. { Je - sus lives! no long - er now Can Thy ter - rors, Death, ap - pall me;
{ Je - sus lives; by this I know, From the grave He will re - call me;

2. { Je - sus lives! to Him the throne High o'er heaven and earth is giv - en;
{ I may go where He is gone, Live and reign with Him in heav - en.

Bright - er scenes at death com - mence; This shall be my con - fi - dence.
God through Christ for - gives of - fence; This shall be my con - fi - dence.

3 Jesus lives! my heart knows well,
Nought from me His love shall sever;
Life nor death, nor powers of hell,
Part me now from Christ forever :
God will be a sure defence :
This shall be my confidence.

4 Jesus lives ! henceforth is death
Entrance-gate of life immortal :
This shall calm my trembling breath
When I pass its gloomy portal.
Faith shall cry, as fails each sense,
Lord, Thou art my confidence.

Golden Harps are sounding.

1. Gold-en harps are sound-ing, An - gel voi - ces ring, Pearl - y gates are

o - pened, O - pened for the King.... Christ the King of glo - ry,

Je - sus, King of love, Is gone up in tri - umph To His throne a - bove.

Golden Harps are sounding.—Concluded.

All His work is end - ed, Joy - ful - ly we sing,

Unison.

Je - sus hath as - cend - ed! Glo - ry to our King!

2 He who came to save us,
    He who bled and died,
Now is crowned with glory
    At His Father's side;
Never more to suffer;
    Never more to die;
Jesus, King of glory
    Is gone up on high.
      All His work, &c.

5 Praying for His children,
    In that blessèd place,
Calling them to glory,
    Sending them His grace;
His bright home preparing,
    Faithful ones for you;
Jesus ever liveth,
    Ever loveth too.
      All His work, &c.

185

183 Jesus Christ is risen To-day.

1. Je - sus Christ is risen to - day, Al - le - lu - ia!

Our tri - umph - ant ho - ly day; Al - le - lu - ia!

Who did once up - on the cross, Al - le - lu - ia!

Suf - fer to re - deem our loss, Al - le - lu - ia!

2 Hymns of praise then let us sing
Unto Christ, our heavenly King.
Who endured the cross and grave,
Sinners to redeem and save.
Alleluia!

3 But the pains which He endured,
Our salvation have procured:
Now above the sky He's King,
Where the angels ever sing.
Alleluia!

The Day of Resurrection.

1. The day of res - ur - rec - tion; Earth, tell it out a - broad!

The pass - o - ver of glad - ness! The pass - o - ver of God!

From death to life e - ter - nal— From this world to the sky,

Our Christ hath brought us o - ver With hymns of vic - to - ry.

2 Our hearts be pure from evil,
　That we may see aright
The Lord in rays eternal
　Of resurrection light;
And, listening to His accents,
　May hear, so calm and plain,
His own *All Hail!*— and, hearing,
　May raise the victor strain.

3 Now let the heavens be joyful!
　Let earth her song begin!
Let the round world keep triumph,
　And all that is therein:
Invisible and visible,
　Their notes let all things blend—
For Christ the Lord hath risen,
　Our joy that hath no end.

185

Alleluia!

1. Al - le - lu - ia! Al - le - lu - ia! The crown is on the
2. Al - le - lu - ia! Al - le - lu - ia! On that bright morn - ing

Vic - tor's brow: Fin - ished is the bat - tle now; Hence with sad - ness;
He a - rose, Bright with tri - umph o'er His foes; Heaven is ring - ing,

Sing with glad - ness, Al - le - lu - ia! A - men.
Earth is sing - ing, Al - le - lu - ia!

3 Alleluia! Alleluia!
Now Jesus Christ hath gone before,
Heaven is open evermore:
Hence with sadness;
Sing with gladness
Alleluia!

4 Alleluia! Alleluia!
Lord, by Thy love we call on Thee,
So from death to set us free,
That our living
Be thanksgiving,
Alleluia! Amen.

186   Let the merry Church-Bells ring.

CHORUS. 1. 2. 3.

1. Let the mer-ry church-bells ring; Hence with tears and sigh-ing;

Frost and cold have fled from spring, Life hath con-quered dy - ing.

Flowers are smil-ing, fields are gay, Sun - ny is the weath - er;

With the ris - en Lord, to - day, All things rise to - geth - er.

2 Let the birds sing out again
  From the leafy chapel,
Praising Him with whom in vain
  Sin hath sought to grapple.
Sounds of joy come loud and clear,
  As the breezes flutter;
"He arose, and is not here,"
  Is the strain they utter.

3 Let the past of grief be past,
  This our comfort giveth—
He was slain on Friday last,
  Yet to-day He liveth.
Mourning hearts must needs be gay,
  Out of sorrow's prison;
Since the very grave can say,
  "Christ, He hath arisen."

187   The World itself keeps Easter Day.

Allegretto.

SOLO.

1. The world it - self keeps Eas - ter Day, And Eas-ter larks are sing-ing, And
2. There stood three Ma - rys   by   the tomb On Eas-ter morn-ing ear - ly, When

Easter flowers are blooming gay, And Eas-ter buds are springing—And Easter buds are
day had scarcely chased the gloom, And dew was white and pear -ly, And dew was white and

The World itself keeps Easter Day.—Continued.

spring-ing, The Lord of all things lives a-new, And all His works are rising too. The
pearl - y: With loving but with err-ing mind, They came the Prince of Life to find. With

Lord of all things lives a-new, And all His works are ris - ing too.
lov-ing but with err - ing mind, They came the Prince of Life to find.

p CHORUS.   *mf*   *f*   *ff*   *ff*

Al-le - lu - ia! Al-le - lu - ia! Al-le - lu - ia!   Praise the Lord! Praise the Lord!

The World itself keeps Easter Day.—Concluded.

3 But earlier still the angel sped,
    His words of comfort giving,
  "And why," he said, "among the dead
    Thus seek ye for the living?"
  The risen Jesus lives again,
  To save the souls of sinful men.
  Alleluia! Alleluia! Alleluia!
    Praise the Lord!

4 The world itself keeps Easter Day,
    And Easter larks are singing,
  And Easter flowers are blooming gay,
    And Easter buds are springing.
  The Lord is risen, as all things tell:
  Good Christians, see ye rise as well.
  Alleluia! Alleluia! Alleluia!
    Praise the Lord!

188   The Golden Gates are lifted up.

1. The gold-en gates are lift-ed up, The doors are o-pened wide,

The King of glo-ry is gone in Un-to His Fa-ther's side.

2 Thou art gone up before us, Lord,
    To make for us a place,
  That we may be where now Thou art
    And look upon Thy face.

3 And ever on our earthly path
    A gleam of glory lies,
  A light still breaks behind the cloud,
    That veiled Thee from our eyes,

4 Lift up our hearts, lift up our minds:
    Let Thy dear grace be given,
  That while we wander here below,
    Our treasure be in heaven.

5 That where Thou art, at God's right hand,
    Our hope, our love may be;
  Dwell Thou in us, that we may dwell
    For evermore in Thee.

Summer Suns are glowing.

1. Sum-mer suns are glow-ing O - ver land and sea, Hap - py light is
2. God's free mer - cy stream-eth O - ver all the world, And His banner

flow - ing Boun - ti - ful and free. Ev - ery-thing re - joic - es
gleam - eth Ev - ery-where un - furled. Broad and deep and glo - rious

In the mel-low rays, All earth's thousand voi - ces Swell the psalm of praise.
As the heaven a - bove, Shines in might vic-to - rious His e - ter - nal love.

3 Lord, upon our blindness,
  Thy pure radiance pour;
For Thy loving-kindness
  Make us love Thee more.
And when clouds are drifting
  Dark across our sky,
Then, the veil uplifting,
  Father, be Thou nigh.

4 We will never doubt Thee,
  Though Thou veil Thy light;
Life is dark without Thee;
  Death with Thee is bright.
Light of Light! Shine o'er us
  On our pilgrim way,
Go Thou still before us
  To the endless day.

190   From East and West, by many a Way.

SOLO.

1. From east and west, by many a way, Where summer breezes
2. For flowers that bloom on hill and plain, For tender showers of

softly play, The children come, this Children's Day,
early rain, For summer fields of ripening grain,

CHORUS.

To praise Thee, Heavenly Father! To praise Thee, Heavenly Father.
We praise Thee, Heavenly Father! We praise Thee, Heavenly Father.

From East and West, by many a Way.—Concluded.

For all this world of life and light, For gol-den day and
For days of pleas-ure sweet and long, For hap-py homes, un-

dew - y night, For shad-ows calm, and sun-shine bright,
-dimmed by wrong, For love that guards us safe and strong,

We praise Thee, Heavenly Fa - ther! We praise Thee, Heavenly Fa - ther!
We praise Thee, Heavenly Fa - ther! We praise Thee, Heavenly Fa - ther!

3 But most for Him who loves us best,
The Saviour Christ, who gently blessed,
The little children on His breast,
  ‖: We praise Thee, Heavenly Father!:‖
In that dear name of Christ the Lord,
Teach us to spread His gracious word,
That all on earth with one accord
  ‖: May praise Thee, Heavenly Father!:‖

Come, ye thankful People, come.

1. Come, ye thankful peo-ple, come, Raise the song of Harvest-Home! All is safe-ly
2. All this world is God's own field, Fruit un-to His praise to yield; Wheat and tares to-

gathered in, Ere the winter storms begin; God, our Maker, doth provide For our wants to
-gether sown; Unto joy or sorrow grown; First the blade and then the ear, Then the full corn

be sup-plied: Come to God's own tem-ple, come! Raise the song of Harvest-Home!
shall ap-pear: Lord of Har-vest grant that we Wholesome grain and pure may be.

3 For the Lord our God shall come,
And shall take His Harvest home:
From His field shall in that day
All offences purge away:
Give His angels charge at last,
In the fire the tares to cast;
But the fruitful ears to store
In His garner evermore.

4 Even so, Lord, quickly come
To Thy final Harvest-Home!
Gather Thou Thy people in,
Free from sorrow, free from sin;
There, forever purified,
In Thy presence to abide;
Come, with all Thine angels, come,
Raise the glorious Harvest-Home!

192   We plough the Fields and scatter.

1. We plough the fields and scatter The good seed on the land, But it is fed and watered

By God's almighty hand; He sends the snow in win - ter, The warmth to swell the grain,

The breezes and the sunshine, And soft re-fresh-ing rain.   All good gifts around us

Are sent from heaven above, Then thank the Lord, Oh thank the Lord, For all   His love.

2 He only is the Maker
  Of all things near and far:
He paints the wayside flower,
  He lights the evening star:
The winds and waves obey Him,
  By Him the birds are fed:
Much more to us, His children,
  He gives our daily bread.
  All good gifts, etc.

3 We thank Thee then. O Father,
  For all things bright and good,
The seed-time and the harvest,
  Our life, our health. our food ;
Accept the gifts we offer,
  For all Thy love imparts,
And, what Thou most desirest,
  Our humble. thankful hearts.
  All good gifts, etc.

193 Raise the Song of Triumph.

f Joyfully.

1. Raise the song of tri-umph, swell the strains of joy, Hymns in praise of
2. Day by day we're passing through this world of care, Year by year ap-
3. Ten-der-ly the Shepherd ev - ery lamb doth guide; Keep us then, dear

Je - sus let our lips em - ploy; As our Sa - viour greet Him,
proach-ing heaven so bright and fair; Old and young to - geth - er
Sa - viour, safe - ly by Thy side; Faith - ful to Thy prom - ise,

grate-ful tri - bute bring. Prais-es to our Captain, prais - es to our King.
join the pil - grim band. Marching on to vic - tory and the prom-ised land.
storms can ne'er dis - may, Might-y Cap-tain, lead us still in Zi - on's way.

ff CHORUS. 1. 2. 3.

For-ward, for-ward! victory be the cry; On - ward, on -ward, banners waving high;

Raise the Song of Triumph.—Concluded.

Join the an-gel cho-rus in the sky, And sing a-loud to Christ our King.

194   Fair waved the golden Corn.

1. Fair waved the gold-en corn In Ca-naan's pleas-ant land,

When, full of joy, some shin-ing morn, Went forth the reap-er band.

2 To God so good and great,
   Their cheerful thanks they pour;
Then carry to His temple gate
   The choicest of their store.

3 Like Israel, Lord, we give
   Our earliest fruits to Thee,
And pray, that long as we shall live
   We may Thy children be.

4 Thine is our youthful prime,
   And life and all its powers ;
Be with us in our morning time,
   And bless our evening hours.

5 In wisdom let us grow,
   As years and strength are given,
That we may serve Thy church below,
   And join Thy saints in heaven.

195 Lord of the Harvest, Thee we hail!

1. Lord of the har-vest, Thee we hail; Thine ancient prom-ise doth not fail;
2. If spring doth wake the song of mirth; If summer warms the fruit-ful earth;

The vary-ing sea-sons haste their round, With goodness all our years are crowned:
When win-ter sweeps the na-ked plain, Or au-tumn yields its rip-ened grain,

Our thanks we pay, This ho-ly day; Oh let our hearts in tune be found.
We still do sing To Thee, our King; Through all their changes Thou dost reign.

3 But chiefly when Thy liberal hand
Bestows new plenty o'er the land,
When sounds of music fill the air,
As homeward all their treasures bear;
 We too will raise
 Our hymn of praise,
For we Thy common bounties share.

4 Lord of the harvest, all is Thine:
The rains that fall, the suns that shine,
The seed once hidden in the ground,
The skill that makes our fruits abound;
 New every year
 Thy gifts appear;
New praises from our lips shall sound.

Now thank we all our God.

1. { Now thank we all our God, With heart and hands and voic - - es,
   { Who wondrous things hath done, In whom His world re - joic - - es;

Who from our moth - er's arms Hath blessed us on our way,

With count-less gifts of love, And still is ours to - day.

2 Oh, may this bounteous God
    Through all our life be near us,
  With ever joyful hearts
    And blessèd peace to cheer us;
  And keep us in His grace,
    And guide us when perplexed,
  And free us from all ills
    In this world and the next.

3 All praise and thanks to God
    The Father, now be given,
  The Son and Him who reigns
    With Them in highest heaven,
  The one eternal God,
    Whom earth and heaven adore,
  For thus it was, is now,
    And shall be evermore.

197   Forward! be our Watchword.

1. For - ward! be our watch - word, Steps and voi - ces joined;

Seek the things be - fore us, Not a look be - hind:

Burns the fier - y pil - lar, At our ar - my's head;

Who shall dream of shrink - ing, By our Cap - tain led?

Forward! be our Watchword.—Concluded.

For - ward through the des - ert, Through the toil and fight;

Ca - naan lies be - fore us, Zi - on beams with light.

2 Forward, when in childhood
  Buds the infant mind:
All through youth and manhood.
  Not a thought behind:
Speed through realms of nature.
  Climb the steps of grace:
Faint not, till in glory
  Gleams our Father's face:
Forward, all the lifetime,
  Climb from height to height:
Till the head be hoary.
  Till the eye be light.

3 Forward, flock of Jesus.
  Salt of all the earth;
Till each yearning purpose
  Spring to glorious birth:
Sick, they ask for healing.
  Blind, they grope for day:
Pour upon the nations
  Wisdom's loving ray:
Forward, out of error.
  Leave behind the night:
Forward through the darkness,
  Forward into light.

4 Glories upon glories
  Hath our God prepared,
By the souls that love Him
  One day to be shared;
Eye hath not beheld them;
  Ear hath never heard;
Nor of these hath uttered
  Thought or speech a word;
Forward, ever forward,
  Clad in armor bright;
Till the veil be lifted,
  Till our faith be sight.

5 Far o'er yon horizon
  Rise the city towers,
Where our God abideth,
  That fair home is ours;
Flash the streets with jasper,
  Shine the gates with gold;
Flows the gladdening river,
  Shedding joys untold:
Thither. onward thither,
  In the Spirit's might;
Pilgrims, to your country,
  Forward into Light.

Brightly gleams our Banner.

1. Brightly gleams our ban - ner, Pointing to the sky, Waving wanderers on - ward
2. Je - sus Lord and Mas - ter, At Thy sa - cred feet, Here with hearts re-joic - ing

To their home on high. Marching thro' the des - ert, Glad-ly thus we pray,
See Thy children meet; Of - ten have we left Thee Of - ten gone a - stray;

CHORUS.

Still with hearts u - nit - ed Sing-ing on our way. }
Keep us, migh-ty Sav - iour, In the nar-row way. } Brightly gleams our ban - ner,

Pointing to the sky, Waving wanderers on - ward To their home on high.

Brightly gleams our Banner.—Concluded.

3 All our days direct us
    In the way we go,
  Lead us on victorious
    Over every foe;
  Bid Thine angels shield us
    When the storm-clouds lower,
  Pardon, Lord, and save us
    In the last dread hour.—Cho.

4 Then with saints and angels
    May we join above,
  Offering prayers and praises
    At Thy throne of love:
  When the march is over,
    Then come rest and peace,
  Jesus in His beauty,
    Songs that never cease.—Cho.

199   Uplift the Banner! Let it float.

1. Up-lift the ban-ner! Let it float Sky-ward and sea-ward, high and wide;
The sun shall light its shin-ing flolds, The Cross on which the Sav-iour died.

2 Uplift the banner! Angels bend
    In anxious silence o'er the sign,
  And vainly seek to comprehend
    The wonder of the love Divine.

3 Uplift the banner! Heathen lands
    Shall see from far the glorious sight,
  And nations gathering at the call,
    Their spirits kindle in its light.

4 Uplift the banner! Let it float
    Skyward and seaward, high and wide;
  Our glory only in the Cross,
    Our only hope the Crucified.

5 Uplift the banner! Wide and high,
    Seaward and skyward let it shine:
  Nor skill, nor might, nor merit ours;
    We conquer only in that sign.

Onward, Christian Soldiers.

1. Onward, Christian sol - diers, Marching as to war, With the cross of Je - sus,

Go - ing on be - fore. Christ, the roy - al Mas - ter, Leads against the foe;

For - ward in - to bat - tle, See His banners go! Onward, Christian sol - diers,

Marching as to war, With the cross of Je - sus, Go - ing on be - fore.
With the cross of Je - sus,

Onward, Christian Soldiers.—Concluded.

2 At the sign of triumph
  Satan's host doth flee :
On then. Christian soldiers,
  On to victory !
Hell's foundations quiver
  At the shout of praise !
Brothers. lift your voices,
  Loud your anthems raise.—Cho.

3 Like a mighty army
  Moves the Church of God ;
Brothers, we are treading
  Where the saints have trod.
We are not divided,
  All one body we,
One in hope and doctrine,
  One in charity.—Cho.

4 Crowns and thrones may perish,
  Kingdoms rise and wane,
But the Church of Jesus
  Constant will remain.
Gates of hell can never
  'Gainst that Church prevail ;
We have Christ's own promise,
  And that cannot fail.—Cho.

5 Onward then, ye people,
  Join our happy throng,
Blend with ours your voices,
  In the triumph-song ;
Glory, laud and honor,
  Unto Christ the King,
This through countless ages
  Men and angels sing.—Cho.

Keep your Colors flying.

1 Keep your colors flying,
  All ye Christian youth,
To Christ's call replying,
  Full of grace and truth.
Rise in strength and beauty,
  In life's morning glow,
Answer to each duty,
  Onward, upward go.

Cho.—Keep your colors flying,
    Stand for God and truth,
  Keep your colors flying,
    All ye Christian youth.

2 Life is all before you
  Where to choose your way,
Keep Christ's colors o'er you ;
  Watch and fight and pray,

With a firm endeavor,
  Every foe defy,
True to Jesus ever,
  Lift your colors high.—Cho.

3 Keep your colors flying,
  Never think of ease;
Sin and self denying,
  Jesus only please.
Not for worldly pleasure,
  Not for worldly fame,
Not for heaps of treasure;
  Live for Jesus' name !—Cho.

4 Keep your colors flying,
  Walk as Jesus did ;
In Him, living, dying,
  Let your life be hid ;
Hoping, trusting ever,
  Breathe this mortal breath ;
You shall live forever,
  Christ has conquered death.–Cho.

201   We march, we march to Victory.

We march, we march to vic - to - ry! With the Cross of the Lord be -

- fore us, With His lov - ing eye look-ing down from the sky, And His

Grt. to 15th with Sw. coup.

$d = 48.$

Sw.   *Grt.*

We march, we march to Victory.—Continued.

all verses except last. *last verse only.*

ho - ly arm spread o'er us, His ho - ly arm spread o'er us. o'er us.

His arm

add Mixtures.

1. We come in the might of the Lord of Light, In cho - ral train to
2. Our sword is the Spir - it of God on high, Our hel - met is His sal -

Reduce to 15th.

We march, we march to Victory.—Concluded.

meet Him, And we put to flight the armies of night, That the
-va - tion, Our ban - ner the Cross of Cal - va - ry, Our

Swell.   *Grt.*

D. C. mf

sons of the day may greet Him, The sons of the day may greet Him. We
watchword. The In - car - na - tion, Our watchword, The In - car - na - tion. We

3 And the choir of angels with song awaits
  Our march to the golden Zion;
For our Captain has broken the brazen gates
  And burst the bars of iron.

4 Then onward we march, our arms to prove,
  With the banner of Christ before us;
With His Eye of Love looking down from
  And His Holy Arm spread o'er us. [above,

210

202   The breaking Waves dashed high.

1. The break-ing waves dashed high   On a stern and rock-bound coast,
2. Not as the conqueror comes,   They, the true-heart-ed came;

The woods against a storm-y sky Their gi-ant branch-es tossed;
Not with the roll of stir-ring drums, Or trump that sings of fame;

The heav-y night hung dark,   The hills and wa-ters o'er
Nor as the fly-ing come,   In si-lence and in fear,

When a band of ex-iles moored their bark On wild New England's shore.
They shook the depths of des-ert gloom With hymns of lof-ty cheer.

3 Amid the storm they sang,
   The stars heard and the sea!
The sounding isles of woodland rang
   With anthems of the free.
The ocean eagle soared
   O'er rolling wave's white foam,
The rocking pines in forest roared,
   To bid them welcome home.

4 What sought they thus afar?
   Bright jewels of the mine?
The wealth of seas, the spoils of war?
   They sought a faith's pure shrine!
Ay, call it holy ground,
   The soil where first they trod,
They left unstained what there they found
   Freedom to worship God,

203   Come let us sing of Fount and Spring.

SOLO.

1. Come let us sing of fount and spring, Of brook - let, stream and
2. Down fall the showers to feed the flowers, And in the sum - mer,
3. Each lit - tle bird whose song is heard Through grove and mead - ow

riv - er; And tune our praise to Him al - ways, The great and gracious Giv - er.
night - ly The blossoms sip with ro - sy lip, The dewdrops gleaming brightly.
ring - ing, At streamlets brink will blithely drink, To tune its voice to sing-ing.

CHORUS.

1.2.3.4. What drink with wa - ter can compare, That na - ture loves so dear - ly? The
5. Then wel-come wa - ter, ev - erywhere, In foun - tain well or riv - er, And

Come let us sing.—Concluded.

sweet - est draught that can be quaffed Is wa - ter spark-ling clear - ly.
as we drink still let us think Up - on the gra-cious Giv - er.

4 The sheep and kine in fallow fields,
 The deer on mountains lonely,
 The neighing steed in sorest need,
 Will drink of water only.

5 Away all drink that man distills
 So fraught with sin and sadness;
 We'll drain the cup that brings no ills,
 The draught of health and gladness.

204   Praise to God, immortal Praise.

1. Praise to God, im - mor - tal praise, For the love that crowns our days;

Boun-teous source of ev - ery joy, Let Thy praise our tongues em-ploy.

2 For the blessings of the field;
 For the stores the gardens yield;
 For the joy the harvests bring,
 Grateful praises now we sing.

3 Flocks that whiten all the plain,
 Yellow sheaves of ripened grain,
 Clouds that drop refreshing dews,
 Suns that genial heat diffuse.

4 All that Spring with bounteous hand
 Scatters o'er the smiling land;
 All that liberal Autumn pours
 From her rich o'erflowing stores.

5 These to Thee, our God, we owe,
 Source whence all our blessings flow:
 And for these our souls shall raise
 Grateful vows and solemn praise.

Praise to Thee, Thou great Creator.

1. { Praise to Thee, Thou great Cre - a - tor, Praise be Thine from ev - ery tongue;
   { Join, my soul, with ev - ery crea - ture, Join the u - ni - ver - sal song.

Fa - ther, source of all com - pas - sion, Pure, un-bound - ed grace is Thine;

Hail! the God of our sal - va - tion, Praise Him for His love di - vine.

2 For ten thousand blessings given,
   For the hope of future joy,
Sound His praise through earth and heaven,
   Sound Jehovah's praise on high:
Joyfully on earth adore Him,
   Till, in heaven, our song we raise;
There, enraptured, fall before Him,
   Lost in wonder, love and praise.

My Country! 'tis of Thee.

1. My country! 'tis of thee, Sweet land of lib - er-ty, Of thee I sing; Land where my fathers died! Land of the pilgrims' pride! From ev-ery mountain side Let freedom ring!

2 My native country, thee—
Land of the noble free—
  Thy name — I love;
I love thy rocks and rills,
Thy woods and templed hills:
My heart with rapture thrills
  Like that above.

3 Let music swell the breeze,
And ring from all the trees
  Sweet freedom's song:

Let mortal tongues awake;
Let all that breathe partake;
Let rocks their silence break,—
  The sound prolong.

4 Our father's God! to thee,
Author of liberty,
  To Thee we sing:
Long may our land be bright
With freedom's holy night;
Protect us by Thy might,
. Great God, our King!

---

1 Gone are those great and good
Who here in peril stood,
  And raised their hymn.
Peace to the reverend dead!
The light that on their head
The passing years have shed
  Shall ne'er grow dim.

2 Ye temples, that to God
Rise where our fathers trod
  Guard well your trust,—

The truth that made them free,
Their scorn of falsehood's plea,
Their cherished purity,
  Their garnered dust.

3 Thou high and holy One,
Whose care for sire and son
  All nature fills!
While day shall break and close,
While night her crescent shows,
Oh, let Thy light repose.
  On our free hills.

Before the Lord we bow.

1. Be - fore the Lord we bow, The God who reigns a - bove,

And rules the world be - low, Boundless in power and love;

Our thanks we bring In joy and praise, Our hearts we raise To heaven's high King.

2 The nation Thou hast blest
May well Thy love declare,
From foes and fears at rest,
Protected by Thy care.
For this fair land,
For this bright day,
Our thanks we pay—
Gifts of Thy hand.

3 May every mountain height,
Each vale and forest green,
Shine in Thy word's pure light,
And its rich fruits be seen !
May every tongue
Be tuned to praise,
And join to raise
A grateful song.

208
God of all Creation.

1. God of all cre - a - tion, An - gels bow be - fore Thee;
2. Spheres that sing while shin - ing, In ce - les - tial cho - rus,

Ev - ery tribe and na - tion Wor - ship and a - dore Thee.
Ev - er are com - bin - ing In Thy prais - es o'er us.

3 Nature, too, rejoices
  In responsive measure,
While her myriad voices
  Swell the song of pleasure.

4 Father! life Thou gavest;
  With Thy pardon seal us;
By Thy grace Thou savest;
  In Thy mercy heal us.

Dust, receive thy Kindred!

1. Dust, re - ceive thy kin - dred! Earth, take now thine own! To
2. Guard the pre-cious treas - ure, Ev - er - faith - ful tomb!

thee this trust is ren - dered; In thee this seed is sown.
Keep it all un - ri - fled, Till the Mas - ter come.

3 Watch the well-loved sleeper,
    Guard that placid form;
  Fold around it gently;
    Shield it from alarm.

4 Clasp it kindly, fondly,
    To cherish, not destroy;
  Clasp it as the mother
    Clasps her nestling joy.

5 Guard the precious treasure,
    Ever-faithful tomb:
  Keep it all unrifled,
    Till the Master come.

Close of School ∴ ∴
∴ ∴ and Evening.

210 Now from the Altar of our Hearts.

1. Now from the al - tar of our hearts, Let in-cense flames a - rise,

As - sist us, Lord, to of - fer up Our even - ing sac - ri - fice.

2 Awake! our love; awake! our joy;
Awake! our heart and tongue;
Sleep not when mercies loudly call;
Break forth into a song.

3 Minutes and mercies multiplied
Have made up all this day;
Minutes came quick, but mercies were
More fleet and free than they.

4 New time, new favors, and new joys
Do a new song require;
Till we shall praise Thee as we would,
Accept our heart's desire.

5 Lord of our time, whose hand hath set
New time upon our score;
Thee may we praise for all our time,
When time shall be no more.

Lord, ever show Thy blessèd Face.

1. Lord, ev - er show Thy bless - ed face, Tho' downward sinks the sun; ...
2. As speeds the moon her si - lent way, Out-pour-ing soft - er beams ; ..

Stand still in heaven, with looks of grace, Tho' he his course hath run ; ...
So shed on us a gen - tle ray, The peace of ho - ly dreams ;

Above the height, In glo - ry bright, Still shines in Thee unfad - ing light. Amen.
That thoughts snow-white, May hallow night, No long-er dark be-neath Thy light.

Lord, ever show Thy blessèd Face.—Concluded.

3 When calmly laid in quiet rest,
   Sweet slumber on our eyes,
   Let angels hover round each breast,
   Our guard till morning rise :
      Sin takes to flight,
      And drops the fight ;
   For Thou art peace as well as light.

4 As sighs our last departing breath,
   And friends in sorrow weep,
   Oh, grant us, Lord, a tranquil death,
   Like this, a restful sleep;
      Then, through Thy might
      Raise us all-bright,
   To view Thee robed in quenchless light.

212   Sun of my Soul, Thou Saviour dear.

1. Sun of my soul, Thou Sav-iour dear, It is not night if Thou be near;
2. When the soft dews of kind-ly sleep My wea-ried eye-lids gent-ly steep,

Oh, may no earth-born cloud a-rise, To hide Thee from Thy ser-vant's eyes.
Be my last thought, how sweet to rest For ev-er on my Saviour's breast.

3 Abide with me from morn till eve,
   For without Thee I cannot live;
   Abide with me when night is nigh,
   For without Thee I dare not die.

Now God be with us.

1 Now God be with us, for the night is clos - ing;
2. Let e - vil thoughts and spir - its flee be - fore us;

The light and dark - ness are of His dis - pos - ing, And 'neath His
Till morn - ing com - eth, watch, O Fa - ther, o'er us; In soul and

shad - ow we to rest may yield us, For He will shield us.
bod - y Thou from harm de - fend us; Thine an - gels send us.

3 Let holy thoughts be ours when sleep o'ertakes us;
Our earliest thoughts be Thine when morning wakes us,
Serve Thee all day; in all that we are doing
Thy praise pursuing.

4 Father, Thy name be praised, Thy kingdom given;
Thy will be done on earth, as 'tis in heaven;
Keep us in life, forgive our sins, deliver
Us, now and ever.

214 Through the Day Thy Love hath spared us.

1. Through the day Thy love hath spared us, Night once more in - vites to rest:

Through the si - lent watch - es guard us, Let no foe our peace mo-lest:

Je - sus, Thou our guar-dian be; Sweet it is to trust in Thee.

2 Pilgrims here on earth, and strangers,
Dwelling in the midst of foes,
Us and ours preserve from dangers;
In Thy love may we repose,
And, when life's short day is past,
Rest with Thee in heaven at last.

223

215   Jesus, tender Shepherd, hear me.

1. Je - sus, ten - der Shep-herd, hear me, Bless Thy lit - tle lamb to-night;

Through the dark-ness be Thou near me, Keep me safe till morn-ing light.

2 All this day Thy hand has led me,
   And I thank Thee for Thy care;
Thou hast clothed me, warmed and fed me,
   Listen to my evening prayer.

3 Let my sins be all forgiven,
   Bless the friends I love so well;
Take me, when I die, to heaven,
   Happy there with Thee to dwell.

216   Suppliant, lo! Thy Children bend.

1. Suppliant, lo! Thy chil-dren bend, Fa - ther, for Thy bless - ing now:

Suppliant, lo! Thy Children bend.—Concluded.

Thou canst teach us, guide, de-fend; We are weak; al - migh ty Thou.

2 With the peace Thy word imparts
Be the taught and teacher blest;
In their lives and in their hearts,
Father, be Thy laws impressed.

3 Pour into each longing mind
Light and knowledge from above;
Charity for all mankind,—
Trusting faith, enduring love.

217   Now the Day is over.

1. Now the day is o - ver, Night is draw - ing nigh. . . .

Shad - ows of the eve - ning Steal a - cross the sky.

Shad - ows of the eve - ning Steal a - cross the sky.

2 Now the darkness gathers,
Stars begin to peep,
Birds and beasts and flowers
Soon will be asleep.

3 Jesus, give the weary
Calm and sweet repose,
With Thy tenderest blessing
May our eyelids close.

4 Through the long night watches
May Thine angels spread
Their white wings above me,
Watching round my bed.

5 When the morning wakens,
Then may I arise
Pure and fresh and sinless
In Thy Holy Eyes.

1. Sav - iour, breathe an eve - ning bless-ing, Ere re - pose our eye -lids seal;
2. Though the night be dark and drear-y, Dark - ness can - not hide from Thee;

Sin and want we come con-fess - ing, Thou canst save, and Thou canst heal.
Thou art He who, ne - ver wea - ry, Watch-est where Thy peo - ple be.

Though de - struction walk a - round us, Though the ar - rows past us fly,
Should swift death this night o'er -take us, And our couch be - come our tomb,

An - gel guards from Thee surround us, We are safe, for Thou art nigh.
May the morn in heaven a -wake us, Clad in light and death - less bloom.

Glory be to God the Father.

1. Glo - ry be to God the Fa - ther! Glo - ry be to God the Son!
2. Glo - ry be to Him who loved us, Washed us from each spot and stain!

Glo - ry be to God the Spir - it! Great Je - ho - vah, Three in One!
Glo - ry be to Him who bought us, Made us kings with Him to reign!

Glo - ry, glo - ry, glo - ry, glo - ry, While e - ter - nal a - ges run!
Glo - ry, glo - ry, glo - ry, glo - ry, To the Lamb that once was slain!

3 Glory to the King of angels!
  Glory to the Church's King;
Glory to the King of nations!
  Heaven and earth your praises bring,
    Glory, glory,
  To the King of glory bring.

4 Glory, blessing, praise eternal!
  Thus the choir of angels sings:
Honor, riches, power, dominion !
  Thus its praise creation brings;
    Glory, glory,
  Glory to the King of Kings!

220   Saviour, again to Thy dear Name we raise.

Voices in Unison.

1. Saviour, again to Thy dear Name we raise, With one accord our parting hymn of praise;

We stand to bless Thee ere our worship cease, Then, lowly kneeling, wait Thy word of peace.

2 Grant us Thy peace upon our homeward way ;
  With Thee began, with Thee shall end the day,
  Guard Thou the lips from sin, the hearts from shame.
  That in this house have called upon Thy name,

3 Grant us Thy peace, Lord, through the coming night,
  Turn Thou for us its darkness into light ;
  From harm and danger keep Thy children free,
  For dark and light are both alike to Thee.

4 Grant us Thy peace throughout our earthly life,
  Our balm in sorrow, and our stay in strife :
  Then, when Thy voice shall bid our conflict cease,
  Call us, O Lord, to Thine eternal peace.

Sweet Saviour, bless us ere we go.

1. Sweet Saviour, bless us ere we go; Thy word in - to our minds in - stil;
2. Grant us, dear Lord, from e - vil ways True ab - so - lu - tion and re-lease;

And make our luke-warm hearts to glow With low - ly love and fer - vent will.
And bless us, more than in past days, With pur - i - ty and in - ward peace.

Stanzas. 1, 2, 3, 4.

Through life's long day and death's dark night, O gen - tle Je - sus, be our Light.

dim. e rall.

3 Do more than pardon; give us joy,
    Sweet fear and sober liberty,
    And simple hearts without alloy,
    That only long to be like Thee.

4 For all we love, the poor, the sad,
    The sinful unto Thee we call;
    Oh let Thy mercy make us glad;
    Thou art our Jesus, and our All.

Once more before we part.

1. Once more be-fore we part, Bless the Re-deem-er's name; Let ev - ery tongue and

heart Praise and a - dore the same. Lord, in Thy name we come, Thy

bless-ing still im-part; We meet in Je - sus' name, In Je - sus' name we part.

2 Still on Thy holy word
    We'll live, and feed, and grow,
Go on and know the Lord.
    And practise what we know.
Now, Lord, before we part,
    Help us to bless Thy name;
Let every tongue and heart
    Praise and adore the same.

223   Lord, dismiss us with Thy Blessing.

1. Lord, dis-miss us with Thy bless-ing, Fill our hearts with joy and peace:

Let us all, Thy love pos-sess-ing, Triumph in re-deem-ing grace:

Oh re-fresh us, Oh re-fresh us, Travelling through this wil-der-ness.

2 Thanks we give, and adoration,
   For Thy gospel's joyful sound:
 May the fruits of Thy salvation
 In our hearts and lives abound,
   May Thy presence
 With us evermore be found.

3 So, whene'er the signal's given,
   Us from earth to call away,
 Borne on angels' wings to heaven,
 Glad the summons to obey,
   May we ever
 Reign with Christ in endless day.

1. A might-y for-tress is our God, A bul-wark nev-er
   Our help-er He a-mid the flood Of mor-tal ills pre-

2. Did we in our own strength con-fide, Our striv-ing would be
   Were not the right man on our side, The man of God's own

fail - - ing; }
vail - - ing. }   For still our an-cient foe Doth seek to

los - - ing, }
choos - - ing. }   Dost ask who that may be? Christ Je-sus

A mighty Fortress is our God.—Concluded.

work us woe, His craft and power are great, And. armed with
it is He, Lord Sa - ba - oth His name, From age to

cru - el hate, On earth is not his e - - qual.
age the same, And He must win the bat - - tle.

3 And though this world, with devils filled,
  Should threaten to undo us,
We will not fear, for God hath willed
  His truth to triumph through us.
    The Prince of Darkness grim,—
    We tremble not for him,
    His rage we can endure,
    For, lo! his doom is sure,
    One little word shall fell him.

4 That word above all earthly powers—
  No thanks to them — abideth,
The spirit and the gifts are ours
  Through Him who with us sideth.
    Let goods and kindred go,
    This mortal life also :
    The body they may kill,
    God's truth abideth still;
    His kingdom is forever.

Words and Music written and composed by Martin Luther, at Coburg, in June, 1530.

To God on High.

To God on high be thanks and praise, Who deigns our bonds to
sev - er; His cares our droop - ing souls up - raise, And
harm shall reach us nev - er; On Him we rest, with faith assured, Of
all that live the migh - ty Lord, For ev - er and for - ev - er.

226   God of our Fathers, by whose Hand.

1. God of our fa-thers, by whose hand Thy peo-ple still are blessed,
2. Through each per-plex-ing path of life, Our wandering foot-steps guide;

Be with us through our pil-grim-age, Con-duct us to our rest.
Give us each day our dai-ly bread, And rai-ment fit pro-vide.

3 Oh, spread Thy sheltering wings around,
   Till all our wanderings cease,
  And at our Father's loved abode
   Our souls arrive in peace.

4 Such blessings from Thy gracious hand
   Our humble prayers implore;
  And Thou, the Lord, shalt be our God.
   And Portion evermore.

227   The Lord is my Shepherd.

A-men.

1. The *Lord* | is my | shepherd || *I* | shall — | — not ' want.

2. He maketh me to lie *down* in | green —| pastures : || He *lead*eth me be- | side the | still — | waters.

3. *He* re- | storeth my | soul: || He leadeth me in the paths of *righ*teousness | for His | name's — | sake.

4. Yea, though I walk through the valley of the shadow of *death*, I will | fear no | evil; || for thou art with me; thy *rod* and thy | staff, they | comfort | me.

5. Thou preparest a table before me in the *pres*ence | of mine | enemies; || thou anointest my head with *oil;* my | cup — | runneth | over.

6. Surely goodness and mercy shall follow me *all* the | days – of my | life; || And I will dwell in the *house* of the | Lord for -| ev - —|er.

228   I will lift up mine Eyes.

A - men.

1. I will lift up mine *eyes* | unto – the | hills, || *from* | whence —| cometh – my | help.

2. My help *cometh* | from the | Lord || *which* | made — | heaven – and | earth.

3. He will not suffer thy *foot* | to be | moved, || *He* that | keepeth – thee | will not | slumber.

4. Behold, *He* that | keepeth | Israel || *shall* | neither | slumber nor | sleep.

5. The *Lord* | is thy | keeper; || The Lord is thy *shade* up-| on thy | right — | hand.

6. The sun shall not *smite* | thee by | day, || *nor* the | moon — | by — | night.

7. The Lord shall pre*serve* thee | from all | evil; || *He* | shall pre -| serve thy | soul.

8. The Lord shall preserve thy going *out* and thy | com - ing | in ; || from this time *forth*, and | even – for -| ev - er -| more.

The syllables and words in Italics should be accented.

INDEX OF TOPICS.

CONTENTS.

No.	HYMN.	POET.	COMPOSER.
42	Ever would I fain be reading	Louise Hensel, 1829.	
9	Every morning mercies new	G. Phillimore	E. J. Hopkins, 1818 —
83	Fairest Lord Jesus	Twelfth Century	12th Century, Harmony, by Willis.
194	Fair waved the golden corn	J. H. Gurney, 1802–1862	James Watson, — 1880.
28	Father, again in Jesus' name	Harriet Whittemore, 1831 —	James Langran, 1835 —
68	Father, hear the prayer.		
143	For thee, O dear, dear country	Bernard of Cluny, 1145	Alfred R. Gaul.
197	Forward, be our watchword	Henry Alford, 1810–1871	Henry Smart, 1812–1879.
190	From east and west	A. E. Curtiss	John W. Tufts.
145	From Greenland's icy mountains	Reginald Heber, 1783–1826	Michael Haydn, 1737–1806.
158	From heaven above	Martin Luther, 1483–1546	Luther Gesangbuch.
219	Glory be to God	Horatius Bonar, 1808 —	John Goss, 1800–1880.
86	Glory be to Jesus	Italian, 17th Century	Latin Melody.
	Glory be to the Father (p. 6)		Henry Purcell, 1658–1695.
	Glory be to the Father (p. 6)		William Russell, 1777–1813.
64	God is love, his mercy brightens	John Bowring, 1792–1872	German Chorale.
208	God of all creation.		
29	God of heaven	Frances R. Havergal, 1836–1879.	
226	God of our fathers	Episcopal Collection	John W. Tufts.
182	Golden harps are sounding	Frances R. Havergal, 1836–1879	Arthur S. Sullivan, 1842 —
206	Gone are the great	John Pierpont	Henry Carey, 1748.
51	Gracious Saviour	Jane E. Leeson, 1842 —	Domenica Cimarosa, 1749–1801.
168	Great God, we sing	Philip Doddridge, 1702–1751.	
176	Hail the day	Charles Wesley, 1708–1788	Wm. H. Monk, 1823 —
84	Hail, Thou once-despised Jesus	John Bakenell, 1721–1819.	
78	Hail to the Lord's anointed	James Montgomery, 1771–1854	Melchior Teschner, 1613.
177	Hallelujah! hallelujah	C. Wordsworth, 1807–1885	Arthur S. Sullivan, 1842 —
2	Hark, hark, my soul	Fred. Wm. Faber, 1815–1863	John B. Dykes, 1823–1876.
16	Hark, hark, the organ	Godfrey Thring, 1823 —	James W. Elliott, 1833 —
153	Hark, the herald angels	Charles Wesley, 1708–1788	F. Mendelssohn, 1809–1847.
80	Hark, the sound	C. Wordsworth, 1807–1885	Joseph Barnby, 1838 —
26	Heavenly Father, send	C. Wordsworth, 1807–1885	Henry Smart, 1812–1879.
63	Heavenly Father, sovereign Lord	Salisbury Collection	F. Mendelssohn, 1809–1847.
180	He is risen	C. F. Alexander, 1823 —	Joachim Neander, 1610–1680.
37	He knoweth all His flock	James Wilson Ward, Jr.	
129	Holy Bible	John Burton, 1773–1822	W. H. Havergal, 1795–1870.
75	Holy Father, heavenly King	Charlotte E. Tonna, 1832	C. H. Rinck, 1770–1846.
69	Holy, holy, holy Lord	Benjamin Williams, 1778	Joh. Seb. Bach, 1685–1750.
55	Holy, holy, holy Lord God	Reginald Heber, 1783–1826	John B. Dykes, 1823–1876.
172	Hosanna we sing	G. S. Hodges	John W. Tufts.
130	How precious is the book	John Fawcett, 1739–1817	Arthur S. Sullivan, 1842 —
38	Hushed was the evening hymn	John D. Burns, 1823–1864	Arthur S. Sullivan, 1842 —
90	I could not do without Thee	Frances R. Havergal, 1836–1879	Jacob Arcadelt, 1557.
133	I love to hear the story	Emily Huntington Miller, 1833 —	E. H. Mehul, 1763–1817.
132	I love to tell the story	Kate Hankey	John W. Tufts.
91	I need Thee	Fred. Whitfield, 1829 —	S. S. Wesley, 1810–1876.
67	In heavenly love abiding	Anna L. Waring, 1820 —	John W. Tufts.
160	In the country	Kate Bartlett	Stephen A. Emery.
98	In the cross of Christ	John Bowring, 1792–1872	L. von Beethoven, 1770–1827.
151	It came upon the midnight	Edmund H. Sears, 1810–1876	Old Eng. Melody arr. by Sullivan.
228	I will lift up mine eyes	Psalm cxxi	Thomas Tallis, 1529–1585.
137	Jerusalem the Golden	Bernard of Cluny, 1145	Alexander Ewing, 1830.
41	Jesus, a child His course began	Vesoli	William Shore.
85	Jesus came, the heavens adoring	Godfrey Thring, 1823 —	Henry Smart, 1812–1879.
183	Jesus Christ is risen	Easter Hymn, 1531	Henry Carey, 1696–1743.
46	Jesus Christ our Saviour	William Whiting, 1825 —	John Baptiste Calkin, 1827 —
53	Jesus, gentlest Saviour	Fred. Wm. Faber, 1815–1863	John W. Tufts.
44	Jesus, holy, undefiled	Mrs. E. Shepcote, 1840	John B. Dykes, 1823–1876.
111	Jesus, I live to Thee	John Austin, 1613–1669	Robert Schumann, 1810–1856.
102	Jesus, I my cross have taken	Henry F. Lyte, 1793–1847.	
181	Jesus lives! no longer now	C. F. Gellert, 1718–1769	Johann Crueger, 1598–1662.
48	Jesus, Lord and Saviour	Fred. Wm. Faber, 1815–1863	C. H. Rinck, 1770–1846.
27	Jesus Lord, we hail Thee	Ray Palmer, 1803 —	John W. Tufts.
92	Jesus, love eternal	J. Angelus, tr. by S. H. Ward.	
108	Jesus, lover of my soul	Charles Wesley, 1708–1788	John B. Dykes, 1823–1876.
40	Jesus, meek and gentle	George R. Prynne, 1818 —	
147	Jesus shall reign	Isaac Watts, 1674–1748	Venua.
215	Jesus, tender Shepherd	Mary L. Duncan, 1814–1840	John B. Dykes, 1823–1876.
52	Jesus, the Shepherd	Thomas Kelley, 1769–1855	Joseph Barnby, 1838 —

238

No.	HYMN.	POET.	COMPOSER.
109	Jesus, the very thought	Bernard of Clairvaux, 1091–1153	John B. Dykes, 1823–1876.
25	Jesus, we Thy promise claim		C. W. von Gluck, 1714–1787.
33	Jesus, when a little child	Sunday-school Hymns.	
117	Just as I am	Charlotte Elliott, 1789–1871	George J. Elvey, 1816 —
200	Keep your colors flying.	J. E. Rankin, D.D.	
76	Lead us, heavenly Father	James Edmeston, 1791–1867	Charles Gounod, 1818 —
186	Let the merry church-bells ring.		
59	Let us with a gladsome mind	John Milton, 1608–1674	E. J. Hopkins, 1818—
72	Lift up to God	Ralph Wardlaw, 1779–1853	Madan's Collection.
223	Lord, dismiss us	Walter Shirley, 1725–1786	Henry J. Gauntlett, 1806–1876.
211	Lord, ever show	R. C. Singleton	Joseph Barnby, 1838 —
	Lord, have mercy (p. 8).		
106	Lord, I confess to Thee	Horatius Bonar, 1808 —	E. J. Hopkins, 1818 —
195	Lord of the harvest	John H. Gurney, 1802–1862.	
20	Lord of the worlds above	Isaac Watts, 1674–1748	John B. Dykes, 1823–1876.
24	Lord, this day Thy children	Wm. W. How, 1823—	John B. Calkin, 1827 —
21	Lord, we come before Thee	Wm. Hammond, — 1783	John B. Calkin, 1827 —
30	Lord, what offering	Jane Taylor	W. A. Mozart, 1756–1791.
71	Love divine, all love excelling	Charles Wesley, 1708–1788	Fr. H. Himmel, 1765–1814.
94	Loving Shepherd	Jane E. Leeson, 1842 —	Old Litany, 13th Century.
119	Much in sorrow, oft in woe	Henry Kirke White, 1785–1806	Arr. by John B. Wilkes.
206	My country, 't is of thee	S. F. Smith	Henry Carey, 1696–1743.
104	My faith looks up	Ray Palmer, 1803 —	W. H. Havergal, 1793–1870.
127	My shepherd will supply	Isaac Watts, 1674–1748	Nicolaus Hermann, — 1651.
96	My soul is filled	Hetta L. H. Ward.	
97	My spirit longs for Thee	John Byrom, 1691–1763	John W. Tufts.
210	Now from the altar	John Mason, — 1694	John F. Burrowes, 1787–1852.
213	Now God be with us	Peter Herbert, — 1571	Fred. F. Flemming, 1778–1813.
196	Now thank we all our God	M. Rinckart, 1586–1649	John Crueger, 1598–1662.
4	Now that the daylight	Ambrose, 340–397	Dimitri Bortinansky, 1783.
217	Now the day is over	Sabine Baring-Gould, 1834 —	Joseph Barnby, 1838 —
32	Now the shades of night	Samson Occum, 1770.	
15	O day of rest	C. Wordsworth, 1807–1885	Arthur S. Sullivan, 1842 —
1	O happy band of pilgrims	Joseph of the Studium	Justin H. Knecht, 1752–1817.
159	Oh come, all ye faithful	Bonoventura, 1221–1274	John Reading, 1677–1764.
131	Oh, could our thoughts	Anne Steele, 1716–1778	Joseph Barnby, 1838—
148	Oh, where are kings	Arthur C. Coxe, 1818 —	William Croft, 1677–1727.
99	Oh, where is He	Thomas T. Lynch, 1818–1871	Giornivichi, 1745–1804.
49	O Jesus, God and man	Fred. Wm. Faber, 1815–1863.	
101	O Jesus, I have promised	John E. Bode, 1816–1874	James W. Elliott, 1816 —
88	O Jesus, Jesus, dearest Lord	Fred. Wm. Faber, 1815–1859.	Louis Spohr, 1784–1859.
77	O Jesus, King	Bernard of Clairvaux, 1091–1153.	
107	O Jesus, Thou art standing	Wm. W. How, 1823 —	E. Husband.
93	O Jesus, Thou the beauty art	Bernard of Clairvaux, 1091–1153	A. R. Reinagle, 1794–1877.
113	O love, that casts out fear	Horatius Bonar, 1808 —	U. C. Burnap.
163	Once in royal David's city	C. F. Alexander, 1823 —	Henry J. Gauntlett, 1806–1876.
222	Once more before we part	Hawker's Collection.	W. H. Havergal, 1793–1870.
200	Onward, Christian soldiers	Sabine Baring-Gould, 1834 —	Arthur S. Sullivan, 1842 —
141	O Paradise	Fred. Wm. Faber, 1815–1863	Joseph Barnby, 1838 —
173	O Sacred Head	Bernard of Clairvaux, 1091–1153	J. H. Schein, 1586–1630.
	Our Father, who art in heaven (p. 7).		
22	Our heavenly Father calls	Philip Doddridge, 1702–1751	Earl of Mornington, 1735–1781.
18	Peace be to this habitation	Charles Wesley, 1708–1788	Samuel Webbe, 1740–1817.
150	Peace on earth	Katharine Lee Bates	John W. Tufts.
57	Praise, my soul, the King	Henry F. Lyte, 1793–1847	Michael Haydn, 1737–1806.
61	Praise the Lord, ye heavens	Richard Mant, 1776–1848	Gerard Cobb.
204	Praise to God	Anna L. Barbauld, 1743–1825	N. S. Heincken, 1830.
205	Praise to Thee	John Fawcett, 1739–1817	Joseph Haydn, 1732–1809.
193	Raise the song	Thomas Crawford, 1886	Thomas Crawford.
161	Ring the bells	Agnes Barney	Arthur H. Browne, 1836 —
105	Rock of ages	Augustus M. Toplady, 1740–1778	Joh. Rosenmüller, 1610–1680
17	Safely through another week	John Newton, 1725–1807	J. H. Deane.
220	Saviour, again to Thy dear name	John Ellerton, 1826 —	E. J. Hopkins, 1813—
103	Saviour, blessed Saviour	Godfrey Thring, 1823 —	Theo. Ed. Aylward.
218	Saviour, breathe an evening blessing	James Edmeston, 1791–1867	Italian Melody.
39	Saviour, like a shepherd	Dorothy A. Thrupp, 1779–1847	John H. Willcox.
95	Saviour, source of every blessing	R. Robinson	French Melody.

www.ingramcontent.com/pod-product-compliance
Lightning Source LLC
Chambersburg PA
CBHW030733280326
41926CB00086B/1284